Southern Lighthouses

"Celebrates the beacons that light the way to the southern coast . . .
fascinating stories."
—*The Island Packet,* Hilton Head, S.C.

"Armchair travelers will enjoy this delightful book."
—*Chattanooga Times*

"Roberts and Jones have created [an] emotional and artistic book."
—*Library Journal*

"Bruce Roberts is the rarest of artists: an original. His images in
Southern Lighthouses will become part of your own recollections
of the beauty of the southern coast."
—*Southern Living* magazine

"Technically excellent, thoughtfully framed shots."
—*Chesapeake Bay Magazine*

"A beautifully illustrated book . . . if you can't get there you can read and dream."
—*The Richmond* (Va.) *Times*

by Bruce Roberts and Ray Jones

SOUTHERN LIGHTHOUSES
Chesapeake Bay to the Gulf of Mexico

NORTHERN LIGHTHOUSES
New Brunswick to the Jersey Shore

WESTERN LIGHTHOUSES
Olympic Penninsula to San Diego

GREAT LAKES LIGHTHOUSES
Ontario to Superior

AMERICAN COUNTRY STORES

STEEL SHIPS AND IRON MEN
*A Tribute to World War II Fighting Ships
and the Men Who Served on Them*

SOUTHERN LIGHTHOUSES

Chesapeake Bay to the Gulf of Mexico

SECOND EDITION

Photographs by Bruce Roberts
Text by Ray Jones

A Voyager Book

The Globe Pequot Press

Old Saybrook, Connecticut

Library of Congress Cataloging-in-Publication Data
Roberts, Bruce.
        Southern lighthouses : Chesapeake Bay to the Gulf of Mexico / photographs by Bruce Roberts ; text by Ray Jones. — 2nd ed.
                p. cm.
        "A Voyager Book."
        Includes bibliographical references.
        ISBN 1-56440-644-X
        1. Lighthouses—Southern States. I. Jones, Ray. II. Title.
VK1024.S66R63   1995
387.1'55'0975—dc20   94-46908
                                                                                                          CIP

Cover and text design by Nancy Freeborn
Text research for second edition provided by Cheryl Shelton-Roberts

Printed in Hong Kong by Everbest Printing Co., Ltd., through Four Colour Imports, Ltd.
Second Edition/Fifth Printing

To the memory of Harry Claiborne and Abbie Burgess and the United States Lighthouse Establishment. They worked to change the darkness along the shore into points of light that gave America the best-lighted coastline in the world.

The Ponce De Leon Inlet Lighthouse on the Atlantic coast of Florida possesses this massive brick base. A staircase of more than 200 steps spirals inside the 175-foot tower.

Bodie Island Lighthouse casts an aura of serenity at sunset.

CONTENTS

A powerful Fresnel lens glows in its birdcagelike lantern room atop the Currituck Beach Lighthouse in Corolla, North Carolina. The lens throws out a focused beam that can be seen from nineteen miles at sea.

INTRODUCTION

History's first great lighthouse was also its tallest. Built in about 280 B.C. on an island in the bustling harbor of Alexandria, the Pharos tower reached 450 feet into the skies of ancient Egypt. Its light, produced by a fire kept blazing on its roof, could probably be seen from up to twenty-nine miles out in the Mediterranean. Mariners needed the Pharos Light because Alexandria stood on the flat Nile Delta, and there were no mountains or other natural features to help them find the city.

Ancient peoples had long made a practice of banking fires on hills and mountainsides to bring their sailors home from the sea. With its artificial mountain, Alexandria pulled in seamen from the entire known world. The delta city became the busiest and most prosperous port in the world, and it remained so for almost 1,000 years. Trading ships from Greece, Carthage, and Rome flocked to the city's wharves to load up with the grain grown in wondrous abundance in fields along the banks of the Nile. The sight of the Pharos Light burning far up near the dome of the sky must have filled the breasts of countless sea captains with awe.

The American South also has a proud city named Alexandria, and it, too, is a port. Like the first Alexandria, it was once the heart of a rich agricultural region. Today, it is a wealthy suburb, located just across the Potomac from the nation's capital. In fact, Alexandria was included within the original boundaries of the District of Columbia, but its citizens preferred to cast their lot with agrarian Virginia. At Alexandria's Jones Point, some five or six miles down the Potomac from the city of Washington, is a stone marking one of the corners of the old, ten-mile-square federal district.

Also at Jones Point stands a small, rectangular building with whitewashed wooden walls, a pitched roof, and a porch. Probably no more than twenty feet high, its appearance suggests a nineteenth-century country schoolhouse. Except for the tiny lantern protruding from its roof, one might never guess that it had anything in common with the Pharos tower of ancient Alexandria. But it does. It is a lighthouse.

Although it has been inactive for decades, the Jones Point Light guided ships into Alexandria, Washington, and Georgetown for more than half a century. Built in 1855, it can now claim distinction as the nation's oldest standing inland lighthouse. In counterpoint to its gargantuan ancestor in Egypt, it is also among the world's smallest lighthouses.

The South has many other lighthouses, some much older than the Jones Point Light. While none reach the extraordinary height of the ancient Pharos tower, many of them are very tall indeed. Built on flat, mostly featureless headlands, they have to be tall to serve effectively as sea marks. The Pensacola Lighthouse rises 160 feet above the Florida sand; the Cape Charles Light in Virginia stands 180 feet above the water; and the Hatteras Tower, the tallest brick lighthouse in America, soars 193 feet above the Outer Banks.

Although it has long been inactive, Jones Point Light is the nation's oldest standing river lighthouse. (Courtesy Ray Jones)

Lighthouses have always been a source of intense fascination for landlubbers as well as sailors. Not only are they interesting as architectural achievements, but penetrating the darkness with their lights, they offer direction—to ships and to the human spirit. No less than for the captain of a Roman grain ship approaching Alexandria's Pharos, our first glimpse of one of the South's towering lighthouses—or even of a midget such as the Jones Point Light—is likely to fill us with wonder.

Lighthouses are always interesting, and each, in its own way, is beautiful. Of course, some are lovelier or can boast more exciting pasts than others. Although quite broad in scope, this book does not attempt to picture or tell the story of every one of the South's many coastal lights. Instead, it focuses on lighthouses of special architectural or historical significance.

Many would say the South's most famous and impressive lighthouse stands on North Carolina's Cape Hatteras. In the following passage, Bruce Roberts describes his first encounter with this giant.

A GIANT STANDS ON LIQUID SAND

My first glimpse of the Cape Hatteras Lighthouse came on a cold winter afternoon in 1961. Crossing the bridge over Oregon Inlet where Pamlico Sound meets the Atlantic Ocean, I drove south over forty miles of rough, narrow road. Warned by the signs posted along the road, I knew that if I hooked a wheel off the pavement, I

The Atlantic Ocean storms the beach at fabled Cape Hatteras. Towering above the sands, the giant lighthouse is in mortal danger of being undercut by the sea.

was in trouble. The sands on Hatteras are almost as liquid as its surf, and an unwary driver can easily bury all four wheels down to the axles. But I was cautious and reached Cape Hatteras safely.

On the drive down, I had not passed another car nor seen another person, and at the cape, I was completely alone except for the old, silent lighthouse itself. Cape Hatteras is separated from the North Carolina mainland by the thirty-mile-wide Pamlico Sound, so if you are alone there, you are really alone. At Hatteras, it's easy to empathize with the lonely sailors who for centuries have passed by the cape and struggled to avoid its shoals.

The Cape Hatteras Lighthouse stands on the outer rim of the North American continent, marking an uncertain boundary between land and sea. Watching the waves pound the beach, it becomes obvious that the land has only a tenuous hold on this place and may have to give it back to the sea at any time. But the ocean's grip on its own domain is also slippery. Reaching from Hatteras several miles out into the Atlantic, the Diamond Shoals are almost as much a part of the land as of the sea. These treacherous shoals are very shallow and have punctured and torn open the hulls of countless ships. The shoals are, in fact, one of the reasons a lighthouse was built here.

The Hatteras Light has saved many ships, though there are some it has not

saved. On the shifting, sandy ocean bottom beyond the cape rest Spanish galleons, which over the centuries have spilled out caches of silver and gold doubloons into the sea. Nearby are the rusting decks of German U-boats and the twisted hulks of British tankers sunk by torpedoes. Farther offshore is the final resting place of the *Monitor,* which sank while being towed past the cape. The Civil War ironclad, nemesis of the Confederate warship *Virginia,* sits upright on the bottom, its single turret still intact. During

A lifeboat tossed up on the sand by the sea is a reminder of the many shipwrecks and lives lost off Cape Hatteras in years gone by. It is likely that this lifeboat came off a tanker sunk by a German submarine during World War II.

World War II, a destroyer mistook the *Monitor* for a German submarine and dropped depth charges on the wreck.

Extinguished by the Civil War, the Cape Hatteras Light was temporarily dark when the *Monitor* sank in 1862, and it was dark now as I got out of my car and walked over the dunes toward the tower. I had come to the Outer Banks on a photography assignment, and I wanted a picture of Hatteras Lighthouse with its light burning. The Hatteras light is automated; it comes on every evening as night approaches. So all I had to do was set up my tripod, ready my camera, and wait for the daylight to fade. Soon, the light would flash on in the lantern almost 200 feet above the sea.

Years ago, the light in the Hatteras tower was focused by a big Fresnel lens imported from France. The lens was made in Paris, its huge glass prisms polished by the hands of orphans and homeless street people. These destitute workers were paid only a few pennies a day to polish the three-sided prisms and the round bull's-eye in the center of the lens. Although manufactured under sweatshop conditions, the Fresnel lenses were a godsend to lighthouse keepers and the mariners they served. Truly ingenious inventions, they could gather up and concentrate every flicker from a whale-oil lamp.

Fresnels came in a hierarchy of sizes, referred to as first-order, second-order, third-order, and so on. Among the standard Fresnels, the first-order lenses were the largest, with an inside diameter of roughly six feet. The smallest were the sixth-order lenses, with an inside diameter of only about one foot. The Hatteras Fresnel was a powerful first-order lens able to project a tightly focused beam of light that could be seen from twenty miles at sea.

But the old Fresnel was now gone. It had been replaced by a more modern light source—an aerobeacon with a 1,000-watt lamp. How appropriate to have an airport beacon in a lighthouse so close to Kitty Hawk, a few dozen miles to the north. Orville and Wilbur Wright would have approved.

At last the darkness came, and the automatic beacon switched on, making its first revolution of the night. A few moments later, I took my first picture of the lighthouse flashing out its message just as it had for almost 160 years. Sailors read the message as a warning: "This is Hatteras—stay clear!"

North of Hatteras is Jockey's Ridge, a huge sand dune looking down on the town of Nags Head. The unusual names of the town and the big dune are reminders that not all guiding lights are trustworthy. It is said that the infamous "Blackbeard" and other pirates tied lanterns to the necks of horses and walked the animals along the crest of the ridge. To sailors at sea, the lanterns seemed to bob up and down like cabin lights on a ship riding the waves. This evil trick lured many unsuspecting captains too close to the shore, where their ships were trapped in the shallows and became easy prey for the pirates. Unfortunately, treachery of this kind has been common throughout history.

Today, however, sailors know they can trust the navigational beacons that shine from our coasts. The Hatteras Light has guided countless thousands of ships safely past the protruding cape and its dangerous Diamond Shoals. Ironically, the lighthouse itself may not be safe. I have photographed the Hatteras Light many times since my first lonely night on the cape, and each time I've visited with my camera, it has seemed to me that the sea has moved closer to the old tower. The waves have been eating up the beach, and soon the ocean may threaten the foundation of the lighthouse.

This is not the first time that the ocean has closed in on the lighthouse. But always in the past, just when the waves seemed about to consume the tower, the water backed away. Now the sea approaches again. Where will it stop this time? In 1987 the National Park Service drew up a plan to mount the 208-foot, 2,800-ton structure on steel rails and move it back from the sea. If that ever happens, I hope to be there to photograph it.

My wife, Cheryl, and I now live on the Outer Banks, and we visit Hatteras often. The lighthouse has outlasted hundreds of other structures on the Outer Banks, and each summer day almost 2,000 people climb to the top. The tourists on the catwalk appear as a garland around this fabled monument, a fitting symbol of the affection between people and America's greatest lighthouse.

Cape Hatteras Lighthouse casts a long seaward shadow onto the sand.

CHAPTER ONE

LIGHTS OF
THE LIBERTY CAPES

Delaware, Maryland, and Virginia

Lights of the Liberty Capes

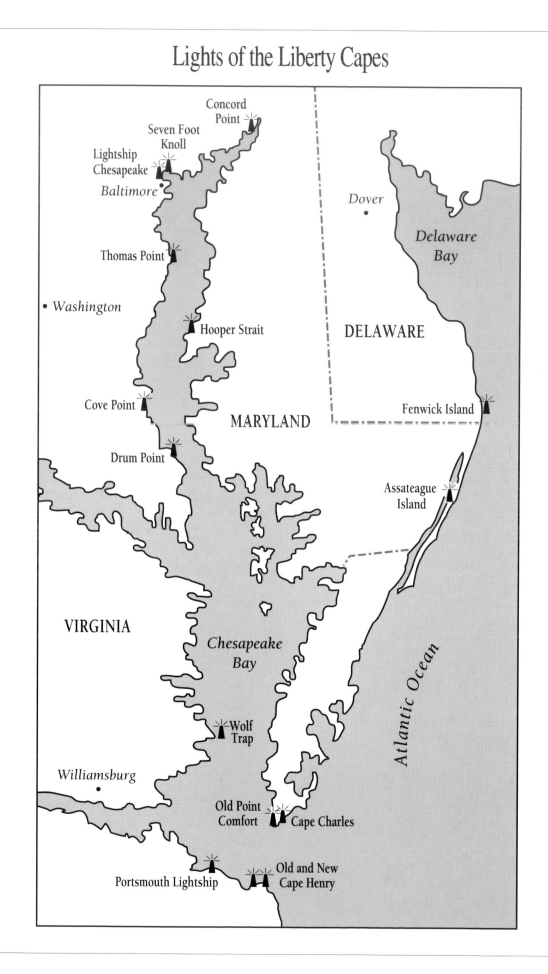

In 1718 Alexander Spotswood, the governor of colonial Virginia, approached the British Board of Trade with a remarkable idea. Why not build a tower on Cape Henry at the mouth of the Chesapeake and place a light atop it to guide ships into the bay? Just such a tower had been built a couple of years before in Massachusetts, and almost overnight, Boston Harbor had become a magnet for sea trade. Spotswood was certain that a similar structure erected on one of the Virginia capes would make the Chesapeake safer for shipping and greatly increase commerce in the region. Spotswood told the British that the benefits of the project seemed to him "so obvious that I have often wondered why so useful a work has not been undertaken long ere now."

The Board of Trade listened politely to the governor's proposal and then proceeded to ignore it. The British government had begun to grow suspicious and, perhaps, a touch envious of the swelling prosperity of its colonies in America. Parliament had no intention of spending good British sterling on a project likely to help the business-minded American colonists make still more money. So the British built no lighthouse on Cape Henry. Three-quarters of a century later, General Charles Cornwallis may have wished they had.

By the mid-1770s British subjects in the American colonies were fed up with their mother country. They hated paying taxes—even a penny a pound on tea—and the negligent attitude of British officials toward needed public projects, such as building lighthouses, made them even more obstinate about opening their purses for the king. It seemed to the colonists that His Majesty George III considered them a lot of country bumpkins. Feeling they were being treated like second-class citizens, increasing numbers of Americans were reaching the conclusion that they must take their destinies into their own hands.

Caught up in the independent spirit sweeping the colonies, the people of Virginia and Maryland decided to pool their resources and build their own lighthouse on Cape Henry. In their view, if the project were left entirely to the British, the mouth of the Chesapeake would be dark forever. But work on the lighthouse had barely started when the alienation of Americans boiled over into open rebellion, and the effort had to be abandoned. Instead of constructing a lighthouse, the colonists now undertook to build a new nation.

By August 1781, when General Cornwallis marched his redcoat army into Yorktown, the British had been fighting for five long years to put down the American revolt. Weary of the struggle, they had sent Cornwallis to America with orders to bring the war to a speedy conclusion. Tough and ruthless, Cornwallis had no scruples at all about burning people's homes and crops and driving off their livestock. He was sent to America to heap misery on the king's unruly subjects, and in a series of destructive sweeps through the Carolinas and Virginia during the spring and summer of 1781, that is exactly what he did. Believing smugly that he had brought the revolutionaries to their knees,

One of several screw-pile lighthouses in the Chesapeake, the Thomas Point Light stands above the bay on its spidery legs. The stone fill on either side of the light is meant to protect it from ice flows. (Courtesy Frank L. Parks)

Cornwallis then fell back to rest and resupply his troops at Yorktown, a small port located conveniently on the banks of the York River near the point where it flows into the Chesapeake.

Cornwallis had one important flaw as a commander—an arrogant disregard for the military prowess of his opponents. He had little respect for the fighting abilities of the French, who had entered the war on the side of the Americans, and even less for George Washington and his ragtag Continental Army. So, even with his back to the York River and the Chesapeake beyond, Cornwallis felt perfectly safe at Yorktown. Indeed, he was so confident that he neglected to hurry his soldiers in their task of fortifying his new base of operations.

It must have astounded the British general to learn, as he did in mid-September, that Washington's army was closing in on Yorktown. Marching alongside the Virginia planter and his Continentals was a large body of French infantry as well as a second American army under Lafayette. Cornwallis realized with a start that he would soon be dangerously outnumbered.

But the general remained calm. He knew he had a resource near at hand that the Americans could not hope to match—the British navy. He had every reason to believe that a fleet of friendly ships would soon appear and, with their massed cannons, send his enemies fleeing into the woods. Cornwallis felt sure that, at the very least, he could count on the Royal Navy to help evacuate his troops.

Exactly as Cornwallis thought, help was on the way; a large British squadron of twenty-seven ships commanded by Admiral Thomas Graves was pushing south under full sail. But the relief squadron never reached Yorktown. Just as Graves cut westward into the Chesapeake at the Virginia Capes, he slammed into an unexpected obstacle: A powerful fleet of thirty-six French warships under Rear Admiral de Grasse blocked the way. Cannons flashed and thundered for hour after hour, and when the battle was over, three British fighting ships had been sunk and the rest were fleeing north in disorder.

Cornwallis's proud redcoats now found themselves tightly squeezed between the Americans and French to their front and the York River at their backs. The British crouched low in their trenches as cannonballs rained in from several directions. The artillery barrage became so fierce that Cornwallis had to move his headquarters into a cave under the bluffs along the Yorktown waterfront. To prevent French ships from sailing into the harbor and shelling him from the rear, Cornwallis created artificial shoals in the river by scuttling his supply boats.

The British fought on for weeks, but with no help coming from beyond the capes, the outcome of the siege was no longer in question. On October 20 a band played a tune called "The World Turned Upside Down," as the redcoats marched out from behind their fortifications and surrendered. The Americans had won the Revolutionary War and with it the right to collect their own taxes and, if they wished, build their own lighthouses.

What course might history have taken if the British had built a lighthouse on the Virginia Capes shortly after 1718, when the colonists first asked for it? Had the British been more solicitous of their colonies, paid closer attention to their needs, maybe there would never have been a revolution in the first place. And even if the split was inevitable, the battle of Yorktown and the war itself might have ended differently. Perhaps a light on Cape Henry would have enabled a relief fleet to slip past the French blockade in the night and rescue Cornwallis.

BY THE DAWN'S EARLY LIGHT

Roughly a dozen years after the Yorktown siege, the United States government built a lighthouse on Cape Henry, the very place where old Governor Spotswood had envisioned a tower and light a lifetime earlier (Spotswood died in 1740). Its fish-oil lamps were first lit one night in October 1792 and were still burning brightly some twenty years later, when British warships returned to the Chesapeake to fight the War of 1812. This time the Royal Navy met far less opposition at the capes than it had in 1781. In fact, the British captains may very well have used the Cape Henry beacon to help them steer their ships into the bay.

The invaders remained in the Chesapeake for more than a year, slamming the door on commerce and terrorizing the population. As the British burned and blasted one bay-side community after another, the Americans fought back bravely but ineffectively with a pitiful array of clumsy barges on which they had mounted field cannon. At Hampton Roads, the British captured Fort Monroe, using as a watchtower the Old Point Comfort Lighthouse, which had been in service for only about a dozen years.

Eventually, the redcoats attacked the city of Washington itself, setting fire to the Capitol and the White House. At Baltimore, the British tried an unsuccessful military experiment, bombing Fort McHenry with rockets launched from small boats in the harbor. Most of the rockets exploded high in the air before they ever reached the fort. The British failed to capture the fort, but the sight of the rockets exploding like fireworks over Fort McHenry inspired Francis Scott Key to write a poem—"Oh, say, can you see . . ."

IRON CLASHES WITH IRON

Almost half a century after Key penned his famous lines, war again swept over the Chesapeake. This time it was a great Civil War, with American fighting American, North against South. Vastly inferior to the Northern side in naval strength, the Southerners were no friends of lighthouses. To make navigation as difficult as possible for Union sailors, the Confederates snuffed out all but a handful of the lights from Virginia all the way to the Mexican border. The Cape Henry Light was extinguished in 1861, the first year of the struggle. It remained dark in 1862, when the Confederates made their boldest attempt to punch a hole in the tight Union naval blockade of the Southern coasts.

On the morning of March 8, 1862, the Confederate States Ship *Virginia* steamed out of the James River and bore down on a squadron of Union frigates anchored in the Chesapeake within sight of the Old Point Comfort Lighthouse at Fort Monroe. Encased in a shell of iron plates two inches thick, the *Virginia* was a fighting ship such as the world had never seen.

Until this strange vessel appeared from around a bend in the James, sailors on the Union frigate *Cumberland* had been doing laundry and hanging their wet uniforms in the rigging to dry in the breeze. They had reason to be relaxed; as far as they knew, the South had no real navy. The last thing they expected was an attack, but incredibly, an attack was coming. There, in plain sight, was the *Virginia* lumbering along at its sluggish top speed of five knots directly toward the *Cumberland*.

The laundry was snatched down out of the rigging, and the crew quickly readied the frigate's guns. The *Cumberland* started firing while the *Virginia* was still three-quarters of a mile away. But to their horror, the gunners on the doomed frigate saw their shots bounce harmlessly off the *Virginia*'s thick armor. They reloaded and fired, reloaded and fired, but there was no stopping the *Virginia*. It kept plowing forward until, with a tremendous shock, it drove a 1,500-pound iron ram into the wooden ribs of the *Cumberland*. Mortally wounded, the Union ship went down swiftly, taking much of her crew with her.

That same day, the *Virginia* also destroyed the frigate *Congress* and drove several other Union vessels aground on the spreading Chesapeake mud flats. Then, with night approaching, the Southerners took their seemingly invincible ship back to the James. But on the following day, they brought the *Virginia* out again, meaning to put an end to the Union blockade once and for all. This time, however, there was a surprise waiting for the Confederates. Directly in the path of the *Virginia* lay a low, turreted vessel described by one astonished Southern sailor as "a cheese box on a raft." But this small ship, its deck continuously washed over by the waves, was no joke. It was, in fact, an ironclad like the *Virginia,* part of a whole new class of fighting ships called "Monitors."

The *Virginia* and the *Monitor* pounded away at one another for hours, but to little effect. Their historic confrontation ended in a draw. Neither would ever be defeated in battle, though within a few months, both would be sunk. The *Virginia* was scuttled by its own crew to keep it from falling into the hands of Union troops who had overrun the Confederate naval yard at Norfolk. The *Monitor* sank in a fierce storm only a few miles south of the Hatteras Lighthouse.

U-BOATS OFF THE CAPES

The Civil War clash of ironclads was not the last time ships would fight near the Virginia Capes. Many times between 1942 and 1945, the keepers of the Cape Henry Lighthouse saw flashes in the night and heard the thunder of exploding torpedoes fired by German submarines. Despite heavy patrolling by the Coast Guard and U.S. Navy destroyers, U-boat "wolf packs" often lurked in the waters beyond the capes.

The wolves were especially hungry during the winter and spring of 1942. On January 30 of that year, the tanker *Rochester* received a torpedo amidships and sank within sight of the Cape Henry Light. Two weeks later, a pair of torpedoes took down the tanker *E. H. Blum,* also near Cape Henry. On March 20 a German submarine sank the tanker *Oakmar.* In April the tankers *David Atwater* and *Tiger* and the freighters *Robin Hood* and *Alcoa Skipper* were all sent to the bottom by U-boats.

The carnage continued at intervals throughout World War II. The Cape Henry keepers would see a flash or hear a rumble and know that yet another vessel had fallen prey to the unseen enemy beneath the waves. There was little the keepers could do but watch, lend life-saving assistance if they could, and keep their light burning.

CONCORD POINT LIGHT
Havre de Grace, Maryland – 1827

Two years after he had built the Thomas Point Lighthouse—and botched the job—John Donohoo won a contract to erect a lighthouse on Concord Point at Havre de Grace. Donohoo completed the thirty-two-foot stone tower in less than a year for $3,500, and this time his work was solid. The tower still stands today, looking very much as it did when its lamps were first lit in 1827.

Take State 155 off I–95 into Havre de Grace and turn left onto Otsego Street. Then turn right onto Saint John's Street and, finally, left again at the sign for Concord Point. If you get lost, remember that the light is near the Susquehanna River in the southeast part of town.

The lighthouse is open for tours Monday through Friday from 10:00 A.M. to 2:00 P.M. from May through October. For more information, contact the Friends of Concord Point Lighthouse, Box 212, Havre de Grace, Maryland 21078; (410) 939–3303.

Originally, the lantern held a set of lamps and sixteen-inch reflectors. Later, these were exchanged for a fifth-order Fresnel lens, among the smallest Fresnels available. Today, the tower displays a fixed green light as a private aid to navigation. It has been automated since the 1920s.

All the keepers of the Havre de Grace Light came from a single family, that of war hero John O'Niel. During the War of 1812, O'Niel had made a quixotic one-man stand against an entire British fleet. Miraculously, he survived and later was rewarded with the post of keeper at the Havre de Grace Light. The job was passed down from one generation of O'Niels to the next. Finally, in the 1920s, the light was automated, and great-grandson Harry O'Niel had to surrender the tower key.

The thirty-two-foot stone tower on Concord Point was completed at a cost of $3,500—in 1827.

SEVEN FOOT KNOLL LIGHT
Baltimore, Maryland – 1855

On August 21, 1933, Maryland was hit by a storm so violent that it destroyed hundreds of homes and boats along the Atlantic coast and in the Chesapeake Bay. Out on the bay the dark red, cheese-box-shaped Seven Foot Knoll Lighthouse was torn by ninety-mile-per-hour winds and pounded by fifteen-foot waves. The lighthouse trembled and shook, but keeper Thomas Steinise was sure it would stand up to the beating, just as it had so many times in the past.

Then, above the roar of the wind, he heard a disturbing sound, the high-pitched signal of a vessel in distress. The call came from the *Point Breeze,* a tug-boat that had been running for the safety of some protective harbor when it was caught and overwhelmed by the waves.

The hapless tug sank within 500 yards of the lighthouse. Facing near-certain death, Steinise lowered the station's twenty-one-foot dory into the chaotic waters and pulled with all his strength for the wreck. For more than two hours, the keeper battled the storm singlehandedly in his open boat. He managed to rescue six members of the drowning crew.

For his part in the dramatic rescue, Steinise was awarded the Congressional Medal for heroism. "Just doing what was right," the modest Steinise told reporters.

Seven Foot Knoll is the oldest surviving example of the Chesapeake's classic screw-pile lighthouses. Completed in 1855, it served mariners as an active light or daymark for more than 130 years. Designed for a third-order lens, it received a fourth-order Fresnel instead. During fog and heavy weather, the keeper sounded a bell.

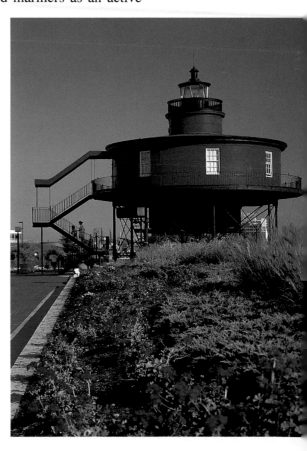

First automated and then put out of service by the Coast Guard, the lighthouse was eventually donated to the City of Baltimore for use as a museum. In 1988 the 220-ton structure was cut from its pilings and carried on a barge to its present location at Pier 5 in the city's popular Inner Harbor district.

From I–95 take the Pratt Street exit and follow the signs to the Baltimore Inner Harbor. There are several parking lots in the area just off Pratt Street. The lighthouse is located near the end of Pier 5. For hours and other information, call (410) 685–0295. While at the Inner Harbor, be sure to visit the nearby lightship Chesapeake. *The Baltimore Inner Harbor offers several excellent restaurants and plenty of intriguing shops. For those interested in undersea life, the National Aquarium, located near Pier 5, is a must-see.*

Shown here on permanent display in Baltimore, the bright red Seven Foot Knoll Lighthouse once marked the entrance to the city's heavily trafficked harbor.

LIGHTSHIP CHESAPEAKE
Baltimore, Maryland – 1930

With an overall length of 133 feet, a 30-foot beam, and a displacement of only 130 gross tons, the *Chesapeake* is a feisty little vessel. Launched in 1930, she guided ships in and out of Chesapeake Bay until World War II, when German U-boats menaced shipping along the eastern seaboard. Fitted with a pair of 20-mm guns, the *Chesapeake* was drafted into the Navy and served out the war as a harbor-patrol boat. Following the war, she became a lightship once again and returned to her original duty station.

From I–95 take the Pratt Street exit and follow the signs to the Baltimore Inner Harbor. There are several parking lots available just off Pratt Street in the Inner Harbor area. The lightship Chesapeake *is berthed in the harbor near the intersection of Pratt and Gay streets. Nearby is the USS* Constellation, *one of the nation's early wooden fighting ships.*

Decommissioned by the Coast Guard in 1971, the hard-working *Chesapeake* became a seagoing environmental classroom for school children. Since 1988, when it was loaned to the City of Baltimore, the ship has provided a different sort of education. As one of the most popular exhibits at the Baltimore Maritime Museum, it reminds visitors of the historic role of lightships in the nation's history.

Now a well-loved fixture of Baltimore's popular Inner Harbor, this famed lightship stood for many years off the Virginia capes marking the entrance to the strategic Chesapeake Bay.

THOMAS POINT LIGHT
Chesapeake Bay, Maryland – 1825, ca. 1840, and 1875

The growth of shipping on the Chesapeake convinced the government to build a small tower on Thomas Point not far from Annapolis. A bank of treacherous shoals extending out into the Chesapeake forced vessels requiring deep water to swing wide around the point. Obviously, a light was needed to help them keep their distance at night. In 1824 federal officials bought seven acres on the point for about $500 and hired a novice contractor named John Donohoo to construct a small tower for about $5,600. The inexperienced Donohoo did a poor job of building the tower, however, and a few years later it had to be torn down and rebuilt.

The contract for reconstruction of the Thomas Point Lighthouse went to Winslow Lewis, who held a patent on the "reflecting and magnifying" lantern used in many American lighthouses (Lewis's system was eventually shown to be inadequate and was replaced in most lighthouses by high-quality Fresnel lenses). Lewis rebuilt the lighthouse for only about $2,500, and his tower guarded the point for more than thirty years. But its light was weak, and Chesapeake sailors grumbled that it was "utterly useless" in fog or foul weather.

In 1875 the Lighthouse Board decided to move the light offshore and place it where it would be most effective—out in the bay, immediately over the shoals. The new lighthouse was a small hexagon-shaped building perched on screw piles. Abandoned, the Lewis tower on the point eventually collapsed, but for more than a century, the light on the shoals has weathered storms, floods, and ice floes—everything that nature has thrown at it. The Thomas Point Light remains active.

The only way to see this lighthouse is by boat. Annapolis, Maryland, is the nearest port. For possible sight-seeing boat tours, contact the Tourism Council of Annapolis and Anne Arundel County, One Annapolis Street, Annapolis, Maryland 21401; (301) 280–0445.

The Thomas Point Light remains on the shoals of Chesapeake Bay, where it has stood since 1875.

HOOPER STRAIT LIGHT
Saint Michaels, Maryland – 1867 and 1879

For more than forty years, beginning in 1827, the crooked channel of Hooper Strait was marked by a lightship. But in 1867 the Lighthouse Board built a modest screw-pile tower there to guide shipping. Ten years later, a massive ice floe swept the little lighthouse off its piles and carried it five miles down the bay. A tender found the wreckage and managed to salvage the lens and some of the equipment.

A larger, hexagonal lighthouse had replaced the crushed tower by the autumn of 1879, and it remained in service for three-quarters of a century. Deactivated in 1954, it was eventually acquired by the Chesapeake Bay Maritime Museum in Saint Michaels on the Maryland eastern shore. In order to move the forty-four-foot-wide structure down the Chesapeake to Saint Michaels, museum officials had it cut in half, like a giant apple, and loaded onto a barge. Reassembled and restored to like-new condition, the lighthouse now stands beside the museum on Navy Point.

After being disassembled and restored, the Hooper Strait Light now stands at the Chesapeake Maritime Museum.

To reach the museum and lighthouse, take US-50 north from Cambridge and then State 33 east to Saint Michaels, a charming Chesapeake Bay community. The museum, which is near the downtown area on Navy Point, is a village in itself, with houses, stores, a restaurant, and wonderful exhibits of small boats used by the bay watermen.

The lighthouse is surrounded by historic workboats and oyster sailboats at nearby docks, giving you the feeling that you have stepped back in time. The Hooper Strait Lighthouse, one of the three remaining screw-pile lighthouses in the Chesapeake Bay, is a cottage-type structure. It was moved to the museum site in 1966 and has been restored and furnished in turn-of-the-century style. If you could only go to one lighthouse, this would be the one to see—even the white-and-red-checkered tablecloth on the kitchen table looks as if the keeper's mug of hot coffee were about to be set upon it.

For more information, contact the Chesapeake Bay Maritime Museum, Box 636, Saint Michaels, Maryland 21663.

Hooper Strait Light, Navy Point

(below) Lighthouse kitchen
(right) Living quarters

DRUM POINT LIGHT
Solomons, Maryland – 1883

Many screw-pile lighthouses once stood in the shallow Chesapeake, but today only a few remain. One of these is Drum Point Lighthouse, a hexagonal, cottage-type lighthouse built on ten-inch, wrought-iron piles.

Erected in 1883, the lighthouse cost $5,000 and took only about a month to build. Fitted with a fourth-order Fresnel lens, it showed a fixed red light, warning vessels of the sandy spit off the point. Having served for almost eight decades, Drum Point Light was taken out of active service in 1962.

Take State 4 south from Washington, D.C., to Solomons. The museum and lighthouse are on the left just before the bridge over the Patuxent River. The lighthouse has been wonderfully restored and furnished in early 1900s style. Small admission fee.

The museum offers exhibits on the paleontology, estuarine biology, and maritime history of the region. For hours and additional information, contact Calvert Marine Museum, Box 97, Solomons, Maryland; (410) 326–2042.

Work room at Drum Point Light

Child's bedroom at Drum Point

(top, opposite page) Close-up of the light at Drum Point
(bottom, opposite page) The Drum Point Light is one of the few remaining screw-pile lighthouses.

COVE POINT LIGHT
Solomons, Maryland – 1828

For the better part of two centuries, mariners navigating the long middle reaches of Chesapeake Bay have watched for the powerful flash of Cove Point Lighthouse. At night the 150,000-candlepower light breaks over the dark waters of the bay every ten seconds. The Cove Point beacon is so bright, in fact, it sometimes disturbs the sleep of nearby residents.

Years ago, a neighbor complained bitterly that the flashing light made it, not just difficult, but impossible for her to get any rest. Several times a minute, all night long, it blasted through her bedroom window turning night into day. Apparently a lady of some influence, she demanded that something be done. To help her rest in peace, keepers hung an opaque curtain in the section of the lantern facing her house. As a result the Coast Guard *Light List* notes that the beacon is obscured from 040 degrees to 110 degrees. Navigators who suddenly and mysteriously lose sight of the light on a dark Chesapeake night might find the explanation interesting.

Among the oldest lighthouses on the Chesapeake, Cove Point marks the entrance to the Patuxent River. The conical, fifty-one-foot, brick tower is the work of John Donohoo, a contractor from Havre de Grace. Donohoo also built the original Thomas Point tower and several other early Chesapeake lighthouses. The Cove Point Lighthouse was among his best, for it has stood intact since 1828.

Erosion threatened the structure almost from the day it was completed. By the 1840s, keepers were reporting severe shore erosion, and retaining walls were built to hold back the bay, enabling the tower to survive at least another 150 years. Today, the Chesapeake has cut to within a few feet of the old tower and may still claim its victim.

Although the light is now automated, Cove Point remains an active Coast Guard station and is off limits to visitors. The area is easily accessible from nearby Solomons, Maryland, however, and the lighthouse can be viewed from the station fence.

Follow Maryland Highway 4 southeast from the Washington, D.C., Beltway to the town of Solomons. Here one can visit the Drum Point Lighthouse before proceeding to Cove Point. From Solomons take Cove Point Road to the Cove Point Coast Guard Station. Best viewing of the light is from about half an hour before sunset until just after dusk. Helpful information may be obtained from the Calvert Marine Museum in Solomons at (301) 326–2042.

Still on active duty, the Cove Point Lighthouse stands watch at a Coast Guard Station. (Courtesy Frank L. Parks)

FENWICK ISLAND LIGHT
Fenwick Island, Delaware – 1858

Fenwick Island Light is actually in Delaware, which was once part of Pennsylvania, but it can be viewed without ever leaving Maryland because the transpeninsular line, an early survey that became part of the Mason-Dixon line, ran through the lighthouse property, separating Delaware and Maryland. In fact, Mr. Mason and Mr. Dixon began their famous survey on Fenwick Island and used the transpeninsular marker, which had been placed years earlier in 1750, as the start of their famous line between the North and the South.

Built in 1858 to guide ships into Delaware Bay, Fenwick Island Lighthouse is eighty-seven feet tall with a focal plane eighty-three feet above sea level. It holds a third-order Fresnel lens. The first painting of the lighthouse's exterior cost the United States government exactly $5.00.

The lighthouse is owned by the state of Delaware and is maintained by the nonprofit Friends of Fenwick Island. The lighthouse is open to the public and depends upon private contributions for most of its maintenance. The light, visible from fifteen miles at sea, fills an otherwise dark gap between the Assateague Light in Virginia and the Cape Henlopen Light to the north.

Although the lighthouse receives some state financial support, it is maintained by volunteers. Interested people are encouraged to join The Friends of Fenwick Island, a nonprofit organization. Fenwick Island Lighthouse is located two blocks west of Route 1 on 146th Street in N. Ocean City, Maryland. The tower is open Memorial Day through Labor Day and at other times by appointment. For more information call or write Paul Pepper, president and founder of The Friends of Fenwick Island Lighthouse, at P.O. Box 6, Selbyville, DE 19975; (410) 250–1098.

The Fenwick Island Lighthouse stands just north of the Mason-Dixon Line, which runs right past the tower.

ASSATEAGUE ISLAND LIGHT
Assateague Island, Virginia – 1833 and 1867

In 1831 Congress appropriated money for a lighthouse to be built a few miles south of the Maryland border on Assateague Island, about halfway between the Chesapeake and Delaware bays. Its chief duty was to warn ships away from the dangerous shoals that extend from the Maryland and Virginia coasts like knife blades; however, after the light was completed and its lamps lit in January 1833, it proved too weak to perform this task effectively. But nothing was done about the problem for almost a quarter century.

Then, during the late 1850s, the Lighthouse Board launched a determined campaign aimed at repairing, upgrading, and correcting the many deficiencies of lighthouses all along the southern coasts. As part of this comprehensive effort, the board decided to rebuild the Assateague Island tower. The Civil War interrupted the work, and the new lighthouse was not ready for service until October 1867. Once its lamps were lit, however, sailors could easily see the improvement. A first-order Fresnel lens made the light visible from nineteen miles at sea.

The Assateague Island Light is now automated but still active. It stands inside the Chincoteague National Wildlife Refuge, not far from the Assateague Island National Seashore.

To reach the Wildlife Refuge from US-13 (the main road down the eastern shore of Virginia), take State 175 to Chincoteague, then follow signs to the refuge across the bridge to Assateague Island. Depending on the season, there may be a small admission fee to enter the wildlife area, which allows hunting. Call (804) 336–6122 for specific information.

Although you can see the lighthouse as you cross the bridge to the island, the tower gets lost behind the trees when you reach land. The person at the tollbooth can provide directions to the tower. A mile or so beyond the tollbooth is a large parking lot on the right side of the paved road. From the parking lot, a trail leads several hundred yards through the woods to the lighthouse.

The tower is painted with red and white stripes and looks something like a candy cane without the curving top. A first-order lens is on display near the base of the tower. The tower itself is closed to the public because the lighthouse is still in service.

Try going to the lighthouse in the late afternoon, and if there are not too many other people in the area, you might see wild deer grazing about the tower as darkness falls.

The Assateague Island Light has been active since 1833.

FORT MONROE OLD POINT COMFORT LIGHT
Fort Monroe, Virginia – 1802

Among the earliest lighthouses constructed in the Chesapeake Bay itself was a stubby, fifty-four-foot tower built in 1802 at Fort Monroe. The light marked the mouth of the James River and the entrance to Hampton Roads.

Because of its strategic location, the lighthouse saw plenty of conflict; several crucial battles were fought within sight of keepers at the lantern. During the War of 1812, British troops under Admiral Cockburn successfully stormed Fort Monroe and later used the lighthouse as a watchtower. Half a century later, the ironclad *Virginia* steamed past the Point Comfort Light on its way to do battle with the *Monitor*. Following the Civil War, Confederate President Jefferson Davis was imprisoned in a Fort Monroe cell not far from the tower.

Fort Monroe remains an active military post and is the home of the Army Training Command. The lighthouse stands in the middle of Officer's Row.

To reach the fort, drive west from Norfolk on I–64; then take the first exit after you emerge from the tunnel under Hampton Road. The sentry at the Fort Monroe gate can provide directions to the lighthouse.

The tower is not open to the public, but visitors are more than welcome at the Casement Museum, located a short distance from the lighthouse. A self-guided tour starting at the museum leads visitors through the historic fort.

Entrance to the fort and museum are free, and both are open daily. For more information, contact the Casement Museum, P.O. Box 341, Fort Monroe, Virginia 23651; (804) 727–3391.

British troops used the Fort Monroe lighthouse as a watchtower during the War of 1812.

LIGHTHOUSES OF CAPE HENRY
Virginia Beach, Virginia – 1792 and 1881

People talked about placing a lighthouse on Cape Henry, at the entrance to the Chesapeake Bay, a long time before anyone actually got around to building one. Among the numerous projects undertaken by Virginia's flamboyant Alexander Spotswood, who governed the colony for the British during the early 1700s, was the construction of a light tower at the mouth of the Chesapeake. Every inch the cavalier, the governor was given to flights of romantic fancy; his ambitious proposals usually generated a great many toasts and a lot of high-toned conversation, but not much action. For instance, in 1716 Spotswood decided to explore the unpopulated wilderness west of the Virginia tidewater, and he actually set off into the backcountry wearing a green velvet riding suit and sporting a sweeping plume in his hat. Spotswood apparently saw his journey into the wilds as something of an extended fox hunt, since he took with him a dozen properly attired Virginia gentlemen and a wagon creaking under a heavy load of wine and liquor. A few days after they had departed, Spotswood and his companions returned to their plantations in much too tipsy a condition to remember anything they had seen.

Spotswood could not interest the British government in his lighthouse idea, but

the governor's proposal attracted numerous advocates in Virginia's House of Burgesses as well as among prominent planters and merchants throughout the Chesapeake region. Like the governor himself, however, they all found it far easier to raise a glass of port than to finance and construct a tall stone tower. Nearly half a century after Spotswood and his plumed hat had passed from the scene, the Cape Henry tower still had not been built.

In 1774 the colonies of Maryland and Virginia finally decided to move ahead with the project. Tons of stone were piled up at the construction site, but funding ran out while the foundation was being laid. Before more money could be found, the drums of the Revolutionary War put a stop to the effort. After the war, stonemasons understandably balked at working for worthless Continental dollars. So, it was not until 1791, shortly after adoption of the Constitution and the establishment of a stable currency, that the project could continue. The nation's first federal Congress authorized a lighthouse for Cape Henry and appropriated $24,077 for its construction.

Contractor John McComb, hired by Secretary of the Treasury Alexander Hamilton, had at first hoped to use the stone stockpiled for the tower by colonial builders twenty years earlier. Unfortunately, most of the big stones had sunk so deeply into the sand that they could not be salvaged. Using freshly quarried sandstone, McComb completed the ninety-foot tower in the fall of 1792.

McComb and his crews built a solid lighthouse; the tower has stood for almost 200 years, through several wars and countless gales. The Confederates put the light out of service briefly at the beginning of the Civil War, but the Lighthouse Board had its lamps burning again by 1863.

In 1870 a network of large cracks began to split the tower. Fearing that the lighthouse would crack open and collapse, the board had a cast-iron tower built about 100 yards to the southeast. Standing 156 feet tall, the new tower received a first-order Fresnel lens and began service to the Chesapeake shipping lanes on December 15, 1881. Both towers still stand today.

Lighthouse towers stand watch at Fort Story.

Both of these lighthouses are located on the grounds of Fort Story at the north end of Virginia Beach. To reach the fort, take US-60 south from Norfolk. The entrance to the fort, an active military post, is about ten miles from downtown Norfolk. The guard at the gate will provide a car pass and directions to the lighthouse.

A National Historic Landmark, the old, 1791 lighthouse is open for visitors to climb the ninety-foot tower every day of the week from March 15 through October 31 from 10:00 A.M. to 5:00 P.M. Children must be at least 7 years old and must be accompanied by an adult. A small admission fee is charged except for military personnel.

For more information, call the Cape Henry Light at (804) 422–9421.

tragic fate of the *Tyrrel*, with the loss of all but one member of its crew, brought heated demands that a lighthouse be erected on Cape Hatteras. But more than forty years and a revolution would pass before a lighthouse was finally built on the cape to guide mariners and warn them away from Hatteras's treacherous shoals.

The lamps of the Cape Hatteras Light were first lit during the summer of 1803. By that time, only a few other lighthouses stood on the sandy coasts and barrier islands of the states south of the Chesapeake, the most notable of them at Cape Fear in North Carolina, Charleston Harbor in South Carolina, and Tybee Island near Savannah, Georgia.

But the Lighthouse Service, formed by act of Congress in 1789, was well aware of the dangers the southern coastline represented to mariners. Obviously, the few lights then in existence were woefully inadequate. Southbound ships had to hug those coasts to avoid fighting the strong northward current of the Gulf Stream. This made them vulnerable to shoals and to being driven ashore by storms. To lessen the dangers, the service (later known as the Lighthouse Board) embarked on a construction program which, after many decades, would dot the southern coasts with tall lighthouses.

CURRITUCK BEACH LIGHT
Corolla, North Carolina – 1875

Its lamps first lit on December 1, 1875, the Currituck Beach Lighthouse illuminated one of the last remaining dark stretches of southern coastline. Strategically placed about halfway between the Cape Henry, Virginia, and Bodie Island lights, the Currituck Lighthouse serves a forty-mile stretch of coast where southbound ships often come perilously close to the shore. Captains keep their ships close-in when heading south in order to avoid the strong northward current of the Gulf Stream.

Because the Currituck tower was built on sand, it was given a strong foundation of heavy timber cribbing. The foundation has remained solid for more than 100 years under the weight of the brick tower, which stands 158 feet above sea level on Whalehead Hill at Currituck Beach. The light from the first-order Fresnel lens is visible from nineteen miles at sea. To distinguish it from the other lighthouses of the Outer Banks, Currituck was to maintain its natural red-brick appearance.

Take US–158 north from Kitty Hawk, and pick up State 12. Continue north on State 12 toward Corolla. The lighthouse will be on the left and can be seen from the road. The tower is open every day from Easter through Thanksgiving from 10:00 A.M. until 6:00 P.M. (5:00 P.M. after daylight saving time ends). It is closed during storms and high winds. For up-to-date information, call (919) 453–1939.

The high-powered light at Currituck Beach is visible from nineteen miles at sea.

CAPE HATTERAS LIGHT
Hatteras Island, North Carolina – 1803 and 1871

America's Mercury and Apollo astronauts were told to watch for the hook of Cape Hatteras when their orbits carried them over the East Coast of the United States. Hatteras is such a prominent feature, it can easily be distinguished, even from hundreds of miles out in space. But earthly mariners have often had a difficult time seeing the cape, especially at night or in foul weather.

Two mighty rivers in the ocean, the cold Labrador Current flowing down from the north and the warm Gulf Stream sweeping up from the Caribbean, pass close by Cape Hatteras. Their strong currents push ships dangerously close to Hatteras and to Diamond Shoals, the shallow bar extending eight miles out into the ocean. As a result, this stormy coast, known to sailors as the "graveyard of the Atlantic," has claimed more than 2,300 ships since the early 1500s.

During colonial times, the British became all too well acquainted with the dangers of Cape Hatteras and her deadly shoals. The ill-fated *Tyrrel* was only one of countless colonial ships that ended their days in the shallows off the coast of North Carolina. But the British Parliament showed little interest in spending money on lighthouses in America, and nothing was done about placing a light on the cape until after the Revolutionary War.

Surfboat rescue crew, Cape Hatteras

Congress authorized construction of the Hatteras Lighthouse as early as 1794, but no brick was laid until late in 1799. The delay was caused, in part, by a political tiff over the selection of a contractor. The job eventually went to Henry Dearborn, a Congressman who would later serve as Secretary of War (the town of Dearborn, Michigan, is named after him). Dearborn's crews, tortured by swarms of mosquitoes and outbreaks of yellow fever, needed three years to complete the ninety-five-foot tower. The light finally went into service in October 1803.

From the beginning, the Hatteras Light had a spotty reputation as a coastal marker. Fitted with eighteen lamps and fourteen-inch reflectors, the light could supposedly be seen from eighteen miles at sea. But ships' captains complained incessantly that they could not see the light, even when nearing the cape. In a report to the Lighthouse Board in 1851, U.S. Navy Lieutenant David Porter called Hatteras "the worst light in the world."

Cape Hatteras Light Station attendants led a spartan life in 1909. Even then, the ocean threatened the existence of the lighthouse. Note the flooding in the foreground. (Courtesy U.S. Coast Guard)

Describing his many journeys around the cape, Porter said: "The first nine trips I made I never saw Hatteras Light at all, though frequently passing in sight of the breakers, and when I did see it, I could not tell it from a steamer's light, except that the steamers' lights are much brighter." In response to Porter's report and to the numerous complaints received about the Hatteras Light, the Lighthouse Board ordered the tower raised to 150 feet and had it fitted with a first-order Fresnel lens.

At the beginning of the Civil War, the Confederates removed the lens and destroyed the lighting apparatus. The Union had the lighthouse back in service again by June 1862, but mariners still considered it inadequate to its task. So, following the war, the board replaced it with a new, 193-foot brick tower, making Hatteras the tallest brick lighthouse in the United States.

The revolving first-order Fresnel lens atop the new tower was in operation by mid-December 1871. Shortly afterward, the old tower was blown up to keep it from falling over in a storm and damaging the new lighthouse or, perhaps, crushing some hapless assistant keeper. After the demolition, the keeper reported sadly that the "old landmark was spread out on the beach, a mass of ruins." The keeper's sentiments aside, sailors agreed that the new lighthouse was a considerable improvement over its predecessor.

The big brick tower, painted with spiral stripes, has stood up to many storms. In 1879 a lightning bolt of extraordinary power opened large cracks in its masonry walls, but the structure remained sound. However, the lighthouse and its keepers soon faced a much more serious threat from beach erosion. By World War I the sea had moved to within 100 yards of the lighthouse. By 1935 high tides brought waves to within a few feet of the foundation. Fearing the water would undercut the structure, officials removed the lens and apparatus, placing them in a skeleton tower erected safely inland. The sea reversed itself, however, and in just a few years' time, replaced much of the beach it had previously gobbled up. By 1950 the Coast Guard thought it safe to reactivate the Hatteras Light. Now automated, the lighthouse is part of the Cape Hatteras National Seashore.

The Hatteras Light can be reached on paved road by taking US-64 at Manteo or US-158 down the Outer Banks past Kitty Hawk to the entrance of the National Seashore. State 12 runs more than forty miles down the barrier dune islands. To reach the lighthouse, turn off State 12 at the village of Buxton. The tower is visible for miles.

Pieces of the Civil War ironclad Monitor *and other bits of "the graveyard of the Atlantic" are on display in a small maritime museum operated by the park service.*

For additional information, contact the Cape Hatteras National Seashore, Route 1, Box 675, Manteo, North Carolina 27954; (919) 473–2111.

This weathered pile of stones is all that remains of the original Hatteras Lighthouse, which was replaced by the present structure following the Civil War. The old, storm-weakened tower was blown up in 1871.

For the past decade, officials have used sand replenishment, sandbag reinforcement, planting of artificial seaweed, steel-groin placement and extension, and a breech-filling riprap to counter nature's assault on the Cape Hatteras lighthouse. These measures will continue in order to keep the lighthouse from being claimed by turbulent waves, the result of a tug-of-war between the southern-flowing, cold Labrador current and the northern-migrating, warm Gulf Stream.

CAPE LOOKOUT LIGHT
Cape Lookout National Seashore, North Carolina – 1812 and 1859

The harbor guarded by Cape Lookout has long been a place of refuge for mariners sailing under the flags of many nations as well as under the skull and crossbones of piracy. Blackbeard is said to have dropped anchor in the harbor. It was used as an anchorage by the British during the Revolutionary War and by the U.S. Navy during two world wars. But the headland protecting this safe harbor from the open sea has always been considered extremely dangerous. Very early on, Cape Lookout earned the title *Promontorium Tremendum,* or "Horrible Headland," by smashing the hulls of ships that strayed too close to its hidden shoals.

Congress authorized a lighthouse for Cape Lookout in 1804, not long after the completion of the Hatteras Light. But as with the Hatteras Light and many other southern lighthouses, there were long delays in construction of the tower, and it was not lighted until 1812. This first Cape Lookout Lighthouse cost $20,678 to build and was of unusual design. It consisted of an inner tower of brick enveloped by an outer cocoon of wood.

Painted with red and white stripes, the tower rose 104 feet above the water, but its light was surprisingly weak. Skippers often had a difficult time seeing it, particularly at night. David Porter, while a mail-steamer captain, complained that on more than one occasion he almost ran up on the shoals while looking for the light.

To improve the light's performance, the Lighthouse Board had a new, 156-foot tower constructed in 1859, fitting it with a first-order Fresnel lens. Confederates retreating from nearby Fort Macon knocked out the lens, but the board quickly replaced it with a third-order Fresnel, and the light remained in service. In 1873 the tower was painted with the unusual diamond pattern that still distinguishes it from other lights today.

To reach the Cape Lookout National Seashore, take US-70 north through Morehead City and Beaufort; at Otway follow the signs to Harkers Island; then follow the paved road to the ferry dock. Twice a day the ferry carries passengers only (no cars) to the barrier island where the lighthouse is located; the ferry leaves Harkers Island at 9:00 A.M. and 1:00 P.M.; the cost is $12 for adults. Be sure to take water, food, and bug spray; there are no facilities on the barrier island.

Maintained by the Coast Guard, the lighthouse is not open to the public. But the trip to the barrier island is still worthwhile—the beaches and island are part of the National Seashore and are kept in their natural state.

For additional information, contact the Cape Lookout National Seashore, 3601 Bridges Street, Station F, Morehead City, North Carolina 28557–2913; (919) 728–2250.

(right) The Cape Lookout Light has warned sailors for years of the dangerous, hidden shoals off the headland.

CHARLESTON LIGHT

Morris Island, South Carolina – 1767, 1837, and 1876

A copper plate inserted in the cornerstone of the Charleston Lighthouse reads, "The First Stone of this beacon was laid on the 30th of May 1767 in the seventh year of his Majesty's Reign, George the III." Built by the British colony of South Carolina a few years after the conclusion of the French and Indian War, the Charleston Lighthouse was for decades the only significant navigational light on the southern coasts of America. Located on Morris Island at the entrance to Charleston Harbor, the lighthouse guided ships first with beacons of burning pitch and oakum, then large tallow candles, and later spider lamps.

With the passage of the Lighthouse Act, among the first measures enacted by Congress under the Constitution, the federal government inherited the Charleston Lighthouse. In 1800 Congress spent $5,000—a princely sum in that day—repairing and fitting it with an updated lighting apparatus. But by 1837 the old lighthouse had been replaced by a tower built on what was then called Lighthouse Island. The new tower, not far from Fort Sumter, stood 102 feet from base to lantern and had a revolving light. It received a first-order Fresnel lens in 1858, less than three years before the outbreak of the Civil War.

In April of 1861, with war on the horizon, the governor of secessionist South Carolina demanded that the federal government surrender the lighthouse along with all other markers and buoys in the harbor. The board gave up the Charleston Light without a fight, but President Lincoln refused to order his troops to abandon nearby Fort Sumter. As a result, the first battle of the fratricidal "War Between the States" was fought practically in the shadow of the Charleston Lighthouse. The Confederates of South Carolina won the battle, forcing Union troops at Fort Sumter to strike their colors.

The sandy island under Charlston Lighthouse has all but disappeared. The copper plate on the base says the tower's cornerstone was laid in 1767.

The Confederates held Charleston for most of the war, but they could not control the seas beyond the city's once busy harbor. The U.S. Navy imposed a tight blockade, and not long after the fall of Sumter, a Union fleet followed the lighthouse beacon into the Charleston Harbor in an effort to take the city by sea. The attacking fleet was driven off by artillery at Fort Wagner and Fort Gregg, both located on Lighthouse Island. Soon after the attack, the Confederates darkened the light.

Although the naval assault on Charleston failed, the blockade of Southern coasts soon began to strangle the Confederacy. Increasingly desperate, the Southerners made a variety of innovative attempts to break the blockade. One of the most dramatic of these efforts took place within sight of the Charleston Lighthouse tower when, on February 17, 1864, the Confederates staged the world's first successful torpedo attack with a submarine. That night, a thirty-five-foot submersible with six men on board sailed out of Charleston Harbor to take on the Union fleet.

Unseen by watchful gunners on the Northern ships, the Confederate submarine closed in on its prey, the Union warship *Housatonic*. Gliding along just below the surface, the submarine pushed a torpedo, tied to the end of a long pole, into the side of the federal ship. The torpedo exploded, blowing a gaping hole in the hull of the *Housatonic*, which sank in a matter of minutes. Apparently, the submarine was blown apart by the explosion. Neither the tiny submersible nor its crew were ever seen again.

When federal forces finally captured Charleston by land invasion in 1865, they discovered that the Charleston Lighthouse tower had been destroyed. The Lighthouse Board soon learned that the neglected harbor itself had also suffered damage in the war; old channels had been silted over and new ones had been opened up by the tides. To guide ships effectively through the radically altered channels, a new light was needed. After some years of indecision the board let a contract for a lighthouse to be built on the site of the old colonial tower.

Begun in 1874, the new tower took two years to build. Workmen drove piles fifty feet into the mud beneath the island, pouring onto them an eight-foot-thick concrete foundation, and on this solid base, they raised a brick tower 161 feet high. The lighthouse, placed in service on October 1, 1876, was indeed well built. It survived a major hurricane in 1885 and the following year, an earthquake, which devastated much of Charleston.

Sometime prior to 1892, the tower was painted black with white bands to make it easier to use as a daymark. Charleston Light on Morris Island was replaced in 1962 by a new lighthouse on Sullivan's Island. The Coast Guard planned to tear down the old tower, but a local citizens group, led by the son of a former Charleston Lighthouse keeper, fought successfully to preserve the structure.

Take US-17 south from Charleston. After crossing the Ashley River, turn left onto State 171 and follow it to Folley Beach. About a block before State 171 ends at the Atlantic Ocean, turn left onto East Ashley Street and follow it for several miles until it ends at the gate to the U.S. Coast Guard station. Leave your car in the parking area about 100 yards from the gate and follow the path over the dunes to the beach. The lighthouse stands about a quarter mile north on a sandbar separated from the island by erosion.

COCKSPUR ISLAND LIGHT

Cockspur Island, Georgia – ca. 1848

The Cockspur Island Light, also known as the South Channel Light, was lit in 1848 along with its companion, the North Channel Light. The two lights guided ships up the Savannah River past Tybee Island, around Elba and Cockspur islands, into Savannah, Georgia.

Like most lights along the Southern coasts, these two lighthouses were darkened by the Civil War. The North Channel Light, built on Oyster Bed Island, did not survive the fighting. But the South Channel Light, located at the eastern end of Cockspur Island, proved luckier. Although it stood in the direct line of fire during the terrific artillery duel between Confederate batteries at Fort Pulaski and the big Union guns on Tybee Island, the South Channel Light escaped the battle without a scratch.

The Cockspur Island Light was relit following the war and continued in service until 1949, when it was permanently retired. After several years of neglect, the lighthouse was deeded to the National Park Service. Restored in 1978, it is now open to the public.

A poignant story is told about Florence Martus, the sister of George W. Martus, who served for many years as keeper of Cockspur Island Light. For most of her life, Florence lived with her brother in a cottage on nearby Elba Island. One

Cockspur Island Lighthouse perches precariously on a declining finger of land.

fine day in 1887, several sailors, whose ship had docked at Savannah, rowed across to Fort Pulaski, where Florence was spending the afternoon with her father. Florence's father, who had fought at Pulaski, offered to give the sailors a tour of the island. While her father reminisced about his Civil War days, Florence caught the eye of one of the seamen.

A handsome young man, the sailor asked if he could call on her. She agreed. He visited Florence three times while his ship was in port, and before he left, he promised to return and marry her.

"I'll wait for you always," she told him. As his ship sailed with the high tide on the morning following their last meeting, Florence stood in front of her cottage and waved a white handkerchief. No one knows if the sailor waved back at her.

Florence's sailor never returned, and for more than fifty years she continued to wave in vain at every passing ship. But having lost the love of a particular seaman, she won the hearts of mariners in general. Every year more and more sailors watched for her handkerchief as they passed her cottage. Often they brought her gifts from distant ports they had visited. One sailor even brought her a llama from Peru.

Take US-80 east from Savannah. The tower can be seen from the US-80 bridge. The lighthouse stands on an oyster bed off Tybee Island, and the adventuresome can reach it by wading or swimming, depending on the tide. The Park Service, however, recommends renting a boat.

A pelican wings his way up the South Channel, marked for more than a century by the Cockspur Lighthouse. Restored by the National Park Service, the tower stands on an oyster bed and is open to adventuresome visitors.

ST. SIMONS LIGHT
St. Simons Island, Georgia – ca. 1810 and 1872

Lighthouse keepers and their assistants were not always the closest of friends. One Sunday morning in March 1880, the St. Simons lighthouse keeper fought with his assistant keeper on the front lawn of the lighthouse and the assistant shot his superior dead. The assistant, who was relieved of his duties, was later acquitted of murder charges.

In 1907 Carl Svendsen, his wife, and their dog, Jinx, moved to the then-almost deserted island to tend the light. The Svendsens happily went about their professional and domestic business, unaware of the death that had taken place there twenty-seven years earlier. Mrs. Svendsen always waited for her husband to clamber down the tower stairs from the light room before she laid dinner on the table. One evening, hearing a heavy tread on the steps, she put out the food as usual. But this time, when the shoes reached the bottom step, her husband did not appear. Jinx barked an alarm and then scampered for safety.

Mrs. Svendsen climbed the lighthouse steps to look for her husband and found him still at the top of the tower. She told him what she had heard, and at first, Svendsen feared his wife had gone daft in the isolation of their lighthouse station. Then, a few days later, he himself heard the phantom footsteps.

The Svendsens lived in the house for twenty-eight years without ever finding an explanation for the bodiless footsteps that never failed to send Jinx into a frenzy.

The original lighthouse was built in 1810 at the southern extremity of St. Simons Island east of Brunswick, Georgia, to mark the St. Simons Sound. Constructed of tabby, the tower was a white, tapered octagonal structure seventy-five feet tall. It was topped by a ten-foot iron lantern lit by oil lamps held in suspension by chains. Serving first as a harbor light, it was raised to the status of a coastal light in 1857 when the Lighthouse Board installed a third-order Fresnel lens.

The tower and all the light-station outbuildings were destroyed by Confederate troops in 1862 as they retreated from the island. Following the war, the board let a contract to build a new station with a 106-foot tower. As was the case with the building of many southern lighthouses, a mysterious sickness—probably malaria—plagued the construction crew. The contractor himself fell ill and died in 1870. One of the bondsmen took charge of construction in order to protect his investment, but he, too, fell victim to illness shortly after his arrival. Despite the lives lost during construction of the St. Simons Light Station, the tower was completed by a second bondsman, and the lamps were lit on September 1, 1872. The new tower, painted white, had a focal plane 104 feet above sea level.

Take the St. Simons Island causeway east from Brunswick; once on the island, take Kings Way to the south end of the island. The lighthouse is located at the end of Kings Way, which turns into Beachview. Take Beachview and turn right onto 12th Street. The lighthouse is two blocks down on the left, with a shopping area and post office nearby. The white tapering tower and the classic keeper's house are some of the best examples of American lighthouse architecture in the South.

There is a small parking area close to the front door of the keeper's quarters, which houses the Museum of Coastal History. There is an admission fee for both the museum and the lighthouse. The climb to the top of the 106-foot-tall tower provides a grand view of the island.

The lighthouse and museum are open daily except Mondays and some major holidays. Call (912) 638–4666 for more information or to arrange a tour.

The St. Simons Light has an interesting past. A lighthouse keeper died there in 1880, and some visitors claim he haunts the lighthouse station.

CAPE KENNEDY (CANAVERAL) LIGHT

Cape Canaveral Air Force Station – 1848 and 1868

Sometimes construction of a lighthouse did more harm than good to shipping. In 1848 the government built a lighthouse to warn ships away from a bank of dangerous shoals extending several miles to the east of Florida's Cape Canaveral. But the brick tower was only sixty-five feet tall, and its light was so weak that mariners were already over the shoals before they could see it. Some ships ran aground on the shoals when their captains brought them too close to shore while searching the landward horizon for the Canaveral Light.

In 1859 the Lighthouse Board tried to correct the situation by raising a second, much taller tower at Canaveral. But construction crews had just started on the foundation when the Civil War put a stop to their efforts. At war's end they went back to work, and the new tower was completed by the summer of 1868. A cast-iron cylinder lined with brick, the tower stood 139 feet above sea level, and its light could be seen from eighteen miles at sea, a distance more than sufficient to keep ships away from the Canaveral shoals.

Like many lighthouses built on the shifting sands of the South's Atlantic coast, this second Canaveral tower was eventually threatened by erosion. Engineers fought back against the encroaching ocean with stone jetties, but the tides kept gaining on the lighthouse. In 1893, with waves crashing within 200 feet of the tower foundation, the board had the structure dismantled and rebuilt more than a mile west of its original location.

Since 1964 the Canaveral Light has been known as Cape Kennedy Lighthouse; the name change honors the fallen U.S. president who committed the country to placing a man on the moon before 1970. Sailors still use the old light to navigate safely around the Canaveral shoals, but for decades now they have often seen other bright lights on the cape—rockets rushing skyward from the nearby Kennedy Space Center.

Still an operating lighthouse, this nineteenth-century navigation marker has flashed its beam across the bows of modern vessels with names such as Mercury, Atlas, Gemini, Titan, and Apollo. The Air Force Station is accessible to the public only by bus tours from Kennedy Space Center. From I–95 or US-1, take the NASA Parkway; turn northeast onto County 3, and follow the signs to the Kennedy Space Center. Not all tours pass by the lighthouse. For more information on tour routes and costs, contact Spaceport USASM, Visitors Center TWS, Kennedy Space Center, Florida 32899; (407) 452–2121.

(right) The Atlas Centaur 9 takes off at Cape Canaveral, within sight of the Cape Kennedy Light.

HILLSBORO INLET LIGHT
Hillsboro Inlet, Florida – 1907

The Hillsboro Inlet Lighthouse was not built in Florida but rather in the Midwest. Constructed by a Chicago company at a cost of $90,000, it was shipped down the Mississippi to St. Louis, where it delighted crowds at the 1904 Exposition. When the Exposition closed, the lighthouse seemed very out of place. Eventually, it was purchased by the government and moved to Hillsboro Inlet, where it began service as a navigational light in 1907. The last beach lighthouse erected in Florida, it marks the northern approaches to Miami.

The lighthouse was anchored by six huge iron piles, a design innovation intended to ease the strain of wind and water on the structure. The lower third of the octagonal pyramid skeleton was painted white and the upper two-thirds painted black, distinguishing it from its redbrick counterparts at Jupiter Inlet and Cape Florida.

At first, the light was fueled by kerosene, which had to be carried by keepers up the 175 steps in the central stair cylinder to the lantern room, 136 feet above mean sea level. The lens rotated on a mercury-filled reservoir and was driven by a clockwork mechanism powered by a weight. The keeper had to raise the weight by hand every half hour.

The Hillsboro Inlet Lighthouse was displayed at the 1904 Exposition in St. Louis.

The light was converted to electric power in the late 1920s and in 1966 was upgraded to 2,000,000 candlepower. The lens makes one complete revolution every forty seconds, with one-second flashes every twenty seconds. Its light can be seen from twenty-five miles away.

During the light's early years, a series of unexplained fires broke out in the area near the tower. After much investigation, it was discovered that the fires had been ignited by sunlight concentrated by the powerful lens. To solve this problem, a shield was constructed on the landward side.

A plaque near the lighthouse commemorates the death of James E. Hamilton, the legendary mailman who walked barefoot on his delivery route from Jupiter Light to Miami. Hamilton drowned in 1887 while trying to bring mail across Hillsboro Inlet.

Hillsboro Inlet, named for the Earl of Hillsboro, who surveyed much of Florida during the 1700s, has been a target for many severe storms and hurricanes. But the lighthouse, with its sturdy pile legs, has stood firm. During the 1960s it successfully weathered Hurricane Donna, which sent a massive tidal surge swirling over the dunes and inundating the lighthouse's base.

Statue of James E. Hamilton, the barefoot mailman who walked his delivery route from Jupiter Light to Miami. He is commemorated because he drowned trying to bring mail across Hillsboro Inlet.

This lighthouse is located on State A1A between Pompano Beach and Boca Raton. Still in operation and maintained by the Coast Guard, it is not open to the public, but the tower can be viewed from the State A1A bridge over the inlet. An even better view can be had from the beach on the south side of the inlet.

CAPE FLORIDA LIGHT

Key Biscayne, Florida – ca. 1825

Not long after the construction of the Key West Light, a sixty-five-foot lighthouse tower was erected at the opposite (northeastern) end of the island chain. Built in 1825 on Cape Florida, some thirty miles north of Carysfort Reef at the northern entrance to Biscayne Bay, the brick tower had walls five feet thick.

Severely damaged during the 1836 Seminole siege, the lighthouse remained out of service for nearly ten years, largely because the Indians made the site too dangerous for repair crews. When reconstruction was finally underway in 1846, workers discovered that the lighthouse had been the victim not only of Indians but also of fraud. Samuel B. Lincoln, the contractor who had built the tower more than twenty years earlier, had given it hollow walls, saving himself nearly 50 percent on the cost of brick.

The reef-laden coast of southeastern Florida had been claiming ships since the area was discovered in 1497 by John Cabot. And now, even with its light burning again, Cape Florida remained deadly. Ship captains complained that, all too often, they could not see the light. So, following a series of disastrous wrecks during the early 1850s, the board raised the tower to 100 feet above sea level, fitting it with a new Fresnel lens.

Relations with the Seminoles were not always hostile. The Indians regularly traded with the keepers and their families; in fact, they occasionally took the hospitality of the keepers a bit too far. One evening, a Seminole came to the lighthouse keeper to barter. Finding everyone in bed, he slipped into bed himself with one of the children where, to the horror of the keeper's wife, he was found the next morning.

The Cape Florida Light rises from a sea of palm fronds.

74

During the Civil War, the lighthouse had a new set of enemies, the Confederates, who destroyed the illuminating apparatus in 1861. Restored in 1866, it remained in service another twelve years, after which it was replaced by a new lighthouse at Fowey Rocks, two miles southeast of Key Biscayne. But the story of the Cape Florida Lighthouse did not end there. During the 1970s the Coast Guard decided to refurbish and recommission it. Coincidentally, the old sentinel was relighted in 1978, exactly 100 years after it had been extinguished.

(above left) Living room of reconstructed keeper's residence
(above right) Door of Cape Florida Light that was attacked by Seminole Indians

Located only a few miles from downtown Miami, this lighthouse is in a tropical setting of coconut palms and Australian pines at the Bill Baggs State Recreation Area. It can be reached by taking the Rickenbacker Causeway from the southern terminus of I–95. After the causeway, follow Crandon Boulevard to the lighthouse; avoid taking the interstate during the rush hour, when the traffic moves at a snail's pace. There is a toll fee to get onto the island and an admission charge to the Bill Baggs State Recreation Area.

Once inside the recreation area, it seems impossible that a major city is nearby; thick woods lead down to a white sand beach. The lighthouse, near the parking area for the beach, has been temporarily closed for renovation, and the entire area is currently blocked off. It will reopen once renovations are completed. For additional information, contact the Cape Florida Light, Bill Baggs State Recreation Area, 1200 South Crandon Boulevard, Key Biscayne, Florida 33149; (305) 361–5811.

LIGHTHOUSES OF THE FLORIDA REEFS

Sand Key Lighthouse – 1827 and 1853

Alligator Reef Lighthouse – 1873

American Shoal Lighthouse – 1880

In 1622 a chain of ship-killing coral reefs extending far out from the tip of Florida destroyed the large fleet of gold-and-silver-laden galleons commanded by Admiral Marquis de Caderieta of Spain. More than 200 years would pass, thousands of ships and sailors would perish, and countless treasures would be lost before any serious effort was made to mark the reefs with lights.

The first such attempts were made in the 1820s with the construction of a sixty-five-foot brick lighthouse tower at Key West and similar structures at Sand Key, Garden Key, and the Dry Tortugas. Particularly important among these was the lighthouse built on Sand Key in 1827. The light marked the southern approach to Key West and the main channel for ships headed around the tip of Florida in the Gulf Stream. A brick tower built on an exposed island of shifting

Supported by an untidy-looking metal skeleton, Sand Key Lighthouse has survived many hurricanes.

sand, the lighthouse had a short career. In 1846 a hurricane utterly destroyed the tower, killing the female keeper, Rebecca Flaherty, and her family.

Following the tragic loss of the lighthouse and its keeper, a lightship served at the Sand Island Station until 1853, when a screw-pile, skeleton-type tower was ready for service. Standing on a solid footing of nineteen piles screwed ten feet down into the island's coral foundation, the lighthouse has successfully weathered hundreds of storms and hurricanes and remains in service to this day. Construction was supervised by General George Meade, who ten years afterward engineered another remarkable accomplishment, the Union victory at Gettysburg.

While the Sand Key Lighthouse has proven quite durable, the island itself has not. The powerful gulf currents have washed away and replaced the island's sands several times over the years. Today, the lighthouse's iron feet stand in water.

Another essential link in the sparkling chain of lights marking the Florida Keys is the iron-skeleton tower at Alligator Reef. In 1821 the U.S. Navy schooner *Alligator* ran aground here after a battle with pirates. The crew blew up the

The beauty of this azure seawater is deceptive. Alligator Reef Lighthouse stands firm on a submerged natural reef that has torn the belly out of many ships and crushed the life out of countless sailors. (Courtesy U.S. Coast Guard)

KEY WEST LIGHT
Key West, Florida – 1825 and 1847

Florida's greatest menace to shipping was its keys, the long chain of low islands curving southwestward from Biscayne Bay. Captains of seventeenth-century Spanish treasure ships called them *Islas de los Martires*, or Islands of Martyrs. Some say the islands were given their foreboding name because they were covered with scrubby, wind-twisted trees that reminded Spanish sailors of the tortured bodies of Christian martyrs. Others say the islands earned the name by taking the lives of so many seamen.

Ships met with disaster in the keys with such regularity that salvaging their cargoes became a lucrative industry, especially after Florida became a U.S. territory. At first, the American-owned salvage boats, called "wreckers," worked out of foreign ports, such as Havana, since they had no convenient base in American waters. Likewise, the navy had no port to use as a base for operations against the pirates who swarmed through the keys and the nearby Bahamas. But the navy located a deep-water harbor at Key West and, in 1822, purchased the island from its Spanish owner, Juan Pablo Salas, for $2,000.

Formerly, Key West had been a stronghold for pirates. Now, almost overnight it grew into a thriving port with a major naval base and large warehouses to store salvaged goods. In 1825 alone almost $300,000 worth of salvage was sold at auction in Key West. That same year the government had a sixty-five-foot lighthouse built on Whitehead Point to mark the entrance to Key West's harbor.

A hurricane swept over Key West in 1846, demolishing much of the town. It also destroyed the lighthouse, killing the keeper along with his entire family. Within a year, workers had replaced the wrecked tower with another about sixty feet tall. A late-nineteenth-century renovation raised the focal plane of the beacon to eighty-five feet above sea level.

Take US-1 south out of Key Largo. This overseas highway runs 100 miles over bridges and keys until it enters Key West and becomes Truman Avenue. The lighthouse is at the intersection of Truman Avenue and Whitehead Street. The tower, as well as a nearby military museum containing lighthouse exhibits, is open daily (except Christmas Day) from 9:30 A.M. to 4:30 P.M. Admission is charged. For more information, contact the Key West Museum, 938 Whitehead Street, Key West, Florida 33040; (305) 294–0012.

(Photo courtesy Cullen Chambers/L. Bloyd)

OLD PORT BOCA GRANDE LIGHT
AND GASPARILLA REAR RANGE LIGHT
Gasparilla Island, Florida – 1890 and 1927

Built in 1890 on Gasparilla Island, Old Port Boca Grande Lighthouse lights the southern stretches of the Florida coast and, some say, marks the grave of a headless Spanish princess. The island is named for José Gaspar, a bloodthirsty pirate with a lusty appetite for gold, silver, and beautiful women. Gaspar's raids on merchant ships netted him many female prisoners, whom he kept on Gasparilla, which he called *Cautiva,* meaning "captive woman."

One of Gaspar's captives, a beautiful Spanish princess named Josefa, turned the tables on the pirate by imprisoning his heart. Gaspar was so stricken with the lady that he begged her to marry him. However, the proud Josefa answered his marriage plea with a curse and spat in his eye. In a fit of rage, the pirate drew his saber and beheaded her. Overwhelmed with remorse, Gaspar buried Josefa's body on the beach where he had murdered her. To remind him of his love for the princess, he kept her head in a jar on his ship. It is said that Josefa's decapitated ghost still walks the island in search of its missing head.

Boca Grande Lighthouse sits on iron stilts above the erosive surf near the mouth of Charlotte Harbor. The lighthouse was abandoned by the U.S. Coast Guard in 1967 and quickly became prey for vandals and the elements. In an effort to preserve it, local residents had the lighthouse transferred from federal to local ownership in 1972. In 1980 it was placed on the National Register of Historic Places.

Gasparilla Island Rear Range Lighthouse

The Gasparilla Island Conservation and Improvement Association began restoring Boca Grande Light in late 1985, with grants from the Bureau of Historic Preservation, the Florida Department of State, and the Historic Preservation Advisory Council. As part of this effort, the Coast Guard reinstalled Boca Grande's crown—the original imported French Fresnel lens—and on November 21, 1986, the old lighthouse was ceremoniously relit for active federal service to navigation. Work continues on the interior, with plans for both an office for the Department of Natural Resources' resident ranger and a local maritime museum.

The iron-pile Gasparilla Island Rear Range Lighthouse, built to the north of Boca Grande Light in 1927, still guides harbor traffic at night. The term *rear range* refers to twin lights, the rear elevated above the front. When a ship can see one directly above the other, the vessel is in mid-channel.

Old Port Boca Grande Light, Florida

To reach the Gasparilla Rear Range and Old Port Boca Grande lighthouses, take I–75 to exit 32 (Toledo Blade Boulevard) to US-41. Turn south onto State 776 in Murdock, and then take State 771 to Placida. Follow signs to the Boca Grande Causeway, which leads to Gasparilla Island. There is a toll of $3.20 per car to cross the bridge. Once on the island, follow signs to the village of Boca Grande and the lighthouses. The Rear Range Light is not open to the public, but there is a special reward for stopping here—a little public beach offering some of the best picnicking, fishing, and shelling on the gulf.

About one mile beyond the Rear Range Light, at the very end of the island, is Old Port Boca Grande Light, also known as the Gasparilla Island Lighthouse. Located in the Florida State Recreation Area, the light is open to the public on the last Saturday of each month from 10:00 A.M. to 2:00 P.M. There is a $2.00 park visitor fee that accommodates up to eight guests.

For more information, contact the Gasparilla Island Recreation Area, P.O. Box 1150, Boca Grande, Florida 33921; (813) 964–0375.

CHAPTER FOUR

LIGHTS OF HURRICANE ALLEY

Florida Panhandle, Alabama, Mississippi, Louisiana, and Texas

Lights of Hurricane Alley

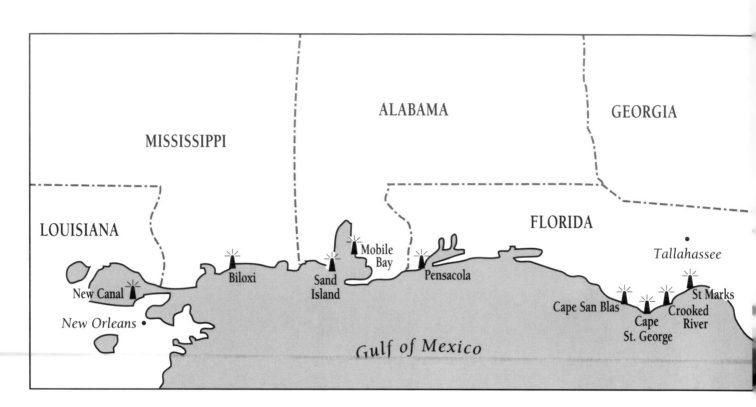

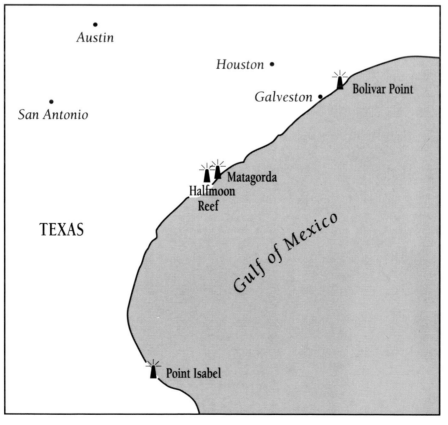

Standing in the gallery of his Bolivar Point Lighthouse on the afternoon of September 7, 1900, keeper Harry Claiborne could see clear signs that trouble was on the way. From his high perch, more than 100 feet above the entrance to Galveston Bay, Claiborne looked down on pristine Texas beaches where, on most days, the blue-green Gulf of Mexico wallowed lazily in the sand. But now the mood of the gulf had changed dramatically. Its waters had turned gray and angry, and it pounded the dunes with enormous waves.

Earlier in the week, when Claiborne had gone into the nearby resort town of Galveston to buy a month's supply of groceries, there was already a hint of uneasiness in people's faces. All summer long the hot, humid air of Galveston Island had buzzed with mosquitoes, but now it vibrated with tension. The weather station on the island had received a distressing cable. Trinidad, on the far side of the Caribbean, had been devastated by a hurricane so powerful that few structures were left standing. It was impossible to say where this deadly storm was now, but sailors arriving at Galveston's bustling wharves brought still more troubling news; they told dock workers, saloon keepers, ladies of the night, and anyone who would listen that they had come through "hell" out in the gulf. Somewhere out there lurked a killer hurricane.

At the turn of the century, meteorologists had no radar or computer-enhanced satellite photos to help them track weather systems; there was no telling where a big storm like this would strike next. It might drift to the east and vent its fury in the empty Atlantic. More likely, however, it would rush northward out of the Caribbean and into the Gulf of Mexico, following a well-traveled path known to sailors as "hurricane alley." In that case, it would threaten all the gulf states from Florida to Texas.

Chances were slim that the storm would hit any one stretch of coastline, so the people of Galveston had no immediate cause for alarm. But then the wind picked up, and high, wispy clouds shaped like fish scales were seen racing westward over the island. The atmospheric pressure started dropping so fast that the barometer at the Galveston Weather Station seemed to have sprung a leak. Seeing these rapid changes, the Weather Bureau put out an emergency forecast—just one word—and editors of the local paper set that word in very large type for their morning editions: HURRICANE.

Strangely, most people ignored the warning. Some even rode out to the island on excursion trains from Houston to witness the natural spectacle firsthand. Throughout the morning of September 8, larger and larger crowds gathered to watch the huge waves slamming into the Galveston beaches. Children squealed with delight and clapped their hands as the big waves crashed down, throwing frothy spray into their faces. It was a tremendous show.

Seeing the big crowd of spectators gathered on the shore, Weather Bureau meteorologist Isaac Cline could not believe his eyes. Was it possible that these

Built in 1831, St. Marks is one of the oldest lighthouses on the Gulf of Mexico.

This third tower was truly a fine piece of work and raised the lantern to a point seventy-three feet above sea level. From this height its fifteen lamps and fifteen-inch reflectors enabled it to be seen by ships more than a dozen miles at sea. The brick-and-mortar tower still stands, despite the violence to which nature and man have subjected it.

During the Seminole Indian Wars, a nervous keeper pleaded for an army detachment to protect the light station—and his scalp. His superiors ignored him and, luckily, so did the rebellious Seminoles. But when the Civil War broke out, the rebels in gray did not ignore the lighthouse. Fearing it would be used to guide Union ships into the strategic St. Marks Harbor, Confederate soldiers tried to blow it up with kegs of gunpowder stacked inside the tower. The blast knocked out a full third of its circumference, but the stubborn tower put on a superb balancing act and refused to fall. Shortly after the war, the Lighthouse Board managed to repair the lighthouse and, by early 1867, had it back in service.

The St. Marks Lighthouse still lights each night and remains among the most picturesque sights on the Gulf Coast. Located in a pristine refuge, alive with seabirds and other wildlife, it is well worth a visit.

Located in the St. Marks National Wildlife Refuge, the lighthouse can be reached by taking State 363 from Tallahassee to St. Marks. Follow signs to the wildlife refuge and take County Road 59 to the lighthouse. The large parking area serves birdwatchers, beach users, and lighthouse visitors.

The tower and keeper's house are open to the public only once a year, sometime in mid-May; group tours can be arranged by writing to Officer in Charge, USCG ANT, Thomas Drive, Panama City, Florida 32407–5898. It is well worth the trip to see this lighthouse, probably the most photographed lighthouse on the Gulf Coast. Birds and alligators abound in the swamps surrounding the lighthouse. Bring your camera.

CROOKED RIVER LIGHT
Carrabelle, Florida – 1895

As early as 1838 a small, isolated light station operated on windy Dog Island, a few miles south of Carrabelle, Florida. For decades, lights there guided freighters into the mouth of the aptly named Crooked River, where they took on valuable loads of hardwood lumber. Then, one day in the fall of 1873, the station keeper looked out into the gulf and saw a mass of black clouds rushing at him from the south. This was no mere gale but a hurricane packing killer winds and a flood tide that soon put the entire island under water. The storm swept the low, sandy island clean, dumping the lighthouse, the keeper's dwelling, and, probably, the keeper himself into the sea. Following this disaster, the board decided not to rebuild the Dog Island Lighthouse.

Lumber boats and freighters, however, continued to pay frequent visits to Carrabelle. By the 1880s this traffic had increased dramatically, and since the Crooked River had a deep entrance, with some eighteen feet of water at the bar, officials saw potential here for a large port. So the board made plans to replace the wrecked Dog Island Light with a mainland lighthouse to be built near the mouth of the river.

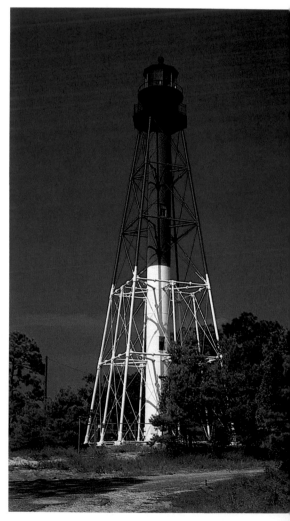

In 1889, the board sought and received $40,000 from Congress to construct a skeleton-style iron tower on the banks of the Crooked River, but the money was not put to use until nearly five years later. Confusion over title to the land and other delays kept workmen away from the construction site until late in 1894. Once underway, though, work progressed so swiftly that the lantern and fixtures were in place by October 1895.

The tower lifted the lantern's fourth-order lens 115 feet above sea level, high enough for the light to be seen from sixteen miles away. The revolving lens showed two flashes every ten seconds. The Crooked River Lighthouse, its lower half painted white and upper half painted dark red, remains in use today.

The lighthouse can be seen from US-98, a few miles west of Carrabelle. A dirt road leads to the tower, located a few hundred yards off the highway. The tower is not open to the public, and there are no facilities of any kind.

CAPE ST. GEORGE LIGHT
St. George Island, Florida – 1833 and 1852

The seventy-foot lighthouse tower on St. George Island had stood for only a few years when a storm came blasting out of the gulf and knocked it down. Rebuilt in 1852, the tower was fitted with a third-order lens that made the light visible more than fifteen miles at sea. This second tower proved much stronger or, perhaps, luckier than the first; it still stands today, despite repeated assaults by hurricanes, gales, and Confederate guns.

During the Civil War, the Confederates fired on the lighthouse and managed to put it out of service temporarily. But the damage was repaired and the light back in use again by the time the war ended in 1865. Not until 1889 did keepers notice a dark, angular crack in the lens, apparently put there by a well-aimed rebel shot.

Marking the western entrance to the Apalachicola Bay, the Cape St. George Lighthouse is in use today. Located on an isolated and uninhabited island, the automated light operates on battery power. The keeper's house and other outbuildings are in ruins, but the tower itself remains as tall and lovely as ever. The island is a fine place to hunt for seashells or, if you like, to be alone for a while.

This isolated lighthouse, no longer an aid to navigation, stands on a remote island that can be reached only by boat. Since the island is not inhabited, visitors should take along drinking water and food. For information and advice on transportation, call the Division of Natural Resources in Apalachicola at (904) 653–9419. To protect the natural turtle habitat, special permission must be obtained to visit the area surrounding the lighthouse.

The Cape St. George Light still stands, despite repeated assaults upon it by nature and man.

CAPE SAN BLAS LIGHT
Cape San Blas, Florida – 1847, 1856, and 1885

A few miles west of the Apalachicola River, the Florida panhandle juts out into the gulf. Here, sand and silt churned up by swirling currents have formed an angular navigational obstacle called Cape San Blas. The same natural process that built the cape also created a series of dangerous shoals extending four to five miles out into the gulf. Constantly shifting and frequently raked by powerful storms, the shoals are a sailor's nightmare. Keeping a light on the cape to warn away ships has likewise proved a nightmare for lighthouse officials.

The Cape San Blas Lighthouse had stood for only four years when, in 1851, it fell in a hurricane—the same giant storm that knocked down the tower at Cape St. George. It took fever-plagued construction crews five years to rebuild the San Blas tower, but its light had shown for only a few months when a gale pushed it over again.

Undeterred, the Lighthouse Board put crews to work once more and had the light back in operation just in time for the Civil War. Confederate raiders hit the cape almost as hard as a hurricane, burning down the keeper's house and torching everything combustible—even the doors and window sashes in the lighthouse tower.

Relighted after the war, the light was in trouble again by the late 1870s. This time the threat was erosion—the gulf was eating away the cape. By 1880 the surf had reached the base of the lighthouse, and with-

The Cape San Blas Light's iron tower was erected in 1885 after it was salvaged from a ship that had sunk.

in two years the tower stood in eight feet of water. Its foundation undermined by seawater, the tower began to settle, leaning further toward the gulf each day. Finally, it could no longer keep its balance and crashed down into the waves.

The board now made plans for yet another lighthouse at Cape San Blas, this one of a type far less susceptible to high winds and water. Instead of a brick-and-mortar tower, it would have a lightweight iron skeleton held together by struts and wires. While the skeleton was under construction at a shipyard in the North, a small light placed on the end of a long pole did the work of alerting ships' crews to the danger of the shoals. This makeshift arrangement continued for longer than anyone had expected, since the ship ferrying the prefabricated skeleton to the gulf sank near Sanibel Island, south of Tampa Bay.

Somehow, the board managed to salvage its iron tower and by 1885 had it in place about 500 feet from the beach on Cape San Blas. But the gulf continued its landward march, often chewing up the cape at the astounding rate of one foot each day. The light had to be moved twice more; eventually the gulf forced the board to move the tower almost a quarter of a mile north.

The Air Force has taken over the land on which the lighthouse is located and has closed it to the public. For any information on when it might be reopened, contact the Apalachicola Bay Chamber of Commerce, 45 Market Street, Apalachicola, Florida 32320.

Since its construction in 1885, the San Blas Light's tower has been moved three times to evade the Gulf of Mexico's erosion upon the shore.

PENSACOLA LIGHT
Pensacola, Florida – 1824 and 1858

Following the acquisition of Florida from Spain in 1819, the U.S. naval presence in the Gulf of Mexico increased dramatically. American warships cruised the dark, sparsely settled coast, discouraging smugglers and flushing out nests of pirates. But with their nearest base on the Eastern Seaboard, literally thousands of sea miles away, these fighting ships and their crews might as well have been operating in foreign waters. In 1824 the U.S. Navy moved to remedy this situation by establishing its first Gulf Coast deep-water base at Pensacola. That same year, a lighthouse was erected to guide warships in and out of Pensacola's excellent harbor, which, with thirty-six feet of water, was one of the deepest on the gulf.

The lighthouse tower was only forty feet tall, but it stood on a forty-foot bluff, giving it an effective height of eighty feet. Even so, sea captains frequently complained that the beam was obscured by tall trees. And the light itself was weak; in 1851 congressional investigators found it "deficient in power, being fitted only with ten lamps and sixteen-inch reflectors." These inadequacies made it little more useful than a small harbor light.

The commandant of the Pensacola Naval Station repeatedly urged Congress to provide the harbor with a "first-class seacoast light." Finally, in 1858, he got his wish. A massive brick tower, built at a cost of nearly $25,000, raised the lantern 210 feet above the sea so that its beacon could be seen up to twenty-one miles at sea.

Only a few years after its construction, the big tower became a target for Union

During the Civil War, the Confederates stole the Pensacola Light's lens and apparatus to incapacitate the Union-occupied light.

gunners firing on Confederate artillerymen dug in around the lighthouse. Unable to keep the lighthouse out of Union hands, the men in gray resorted to the tactic of stealing the lens and apparatus. These were hidden and not found until after the war.

The tower has also withstood bombardment by nature. It has been struck countless times by lightning; in 1875 a pair of bolts seared the lantern, melting and fusing metal parts in the apparatus. Ten years later an earthquake shook the structure so hard that the keeper imagined "people were ascending the steps, making as much noise as possible."

Despite the poundings it has taken, the Pensacola Lighthouse still stands. With its bottom third painted white and its top two-thirds painted black, the tower looks much as it has for more than 100 years. Its light, now automated, continues to lead navy ships and Coast Guard cutters into Pensacola Harbor.

This first-order lens illuminates the Pensacola Light.

The lighthouse, located at the Pensacola Naval Air Station, can be reached by taking Navy Boulevard (State 295) south out of Pensacola. The station is an open post, and the guard at the gate can provide a car pass and directions to the lighthouse. Although the tower and the keeper's quarters are not open to the public, visitors can tour the grounds, which are open daily (except holidays) from 9:00 A.M. to 5:00 P.M. The lighthouse complex has several other buildings, which were used to store lamp oil and supplies. The complex is in remarkably good condition, probably because it has been protected on the base and maintained by the Coast Guard.

MOBILE BAY LIGHT
Mobile Bay, Alabama – 1885

Built in a style used frequently in the Chesapeake Bay, the Mobile Bay Lighthouse consists of a hexagon-shaped cottage with a lantern perched atop its roof. The structure rests on iron pilings screwed into the muddy floor of the bay.

Although quite similar in style, the Mobile Bay Lighthouse proved much more difficult to build than its cousins in the Chesapeake. The iron skeleton that was to hold the lighthouse above the shallow waters of the bay was prefabricated in the North and shipped by sea to Alabama without incident. The trouble began when crews had to erect the skeleton on its pilings far out in the bay. Located in very middle of the bay, the construction site was exposed to the worst weather the gulf could throw at it. Gales hindered crews, and on more than one occasion workmen had to flee for their lives to the Alabama mainland.

While still under construction, the lighthouse began to sink into the sticky mud at the bottom of the bay. Before long, it had lost more than seven feet of its height; but since the settling was evenly distributed, the structure remained sound. The board ordered the light placed in service, and it first shined on December 1, 1885, displaying a white light with red flashes every thirty seconds.

Although five additional lighthouses were planned to mark the serpentine channels through the bay, no more were built. The original cottage lighthouse has stood now for more than a century, a lone sentinel at the heart of Mobile Bay. Although its lamp has been extinguished for many years, ships continue to use the Mobile Bay Lighthouse as a daymark. The Coast Guard intended to demolish the structure in 1967, but spirited public opposition prevented its removal.

Located in the harbor, the lighthouse can only be reached by boat. It is still used as a daymark for ship traffic in and out of Mobile. For updated information, contact the Aids to Navigation Team at the Coast Guard headquarters; (205) 441–6019, ext. 6244.

Although inoperable for many years, the Mobile Bay Light is still a decorative addition to Alabama's coast.

SAND ISLAND LIGHT
Mobile Bay, Alabama – 1838, 1859, and 1872

The island for which this lighthouse was named no longer exists and, for that matter, neither does the light itself. The island long ago eroded and washed away, but the light was extinguished only recently—by a flood of modern shipboard navigational aids that made it unnecessary. Abandoned, isolated, and completely surrounded by the inky waters of Mobile Bay, the black Sand Island tower stands today only as a monument to its own violent and tragic past.

A fifty-five-foot tower was raised on the island in 1838 as a complement to the Mobile Point Light on the opposite side of the entrance to Mobile Bay. Relatively small for a coastal lighthouse, it eventually proved unequal to its task, and plans were made to erect a much larger structure in its place. When completed in 1859, at a cost of $35,000, the new, 150-foot tower was crowned with a first-order lens that probably made the light visible from more than twenty miles at sea.

But the big lighthouse stood for only two years. In 1861 Confederate soldiers noticed Union spotters using the lighthouse to spy on their gun emplacements at Fort Morgan. Under cover of darkness, a rebel raiding party rowed out to the island and blew up the tower, toppling it into the bay.

After the lighthouse was rebuilt during 1871–72 by a yellow fever–tormented work crew, the island beneath the structure began to erode. By 1896 the island beneath Alabama's first and only coastal lighthouse had completely disappeared. During the next ten years, the island reappeared several times, only to vanish in the next storm. Then, in 1906, a hurricane washed it away forever.

Unfortunately, the storm carried away more than just the sand. After the hurricane had passed inland and the winds had died down, a worried lighthouse inspector hurried out to check on the Sand Island Light station and its keepers. Later, the inspector sent this telegram to his superiors: "Sand Island Light out. Island washed away. Dwelling gone. Keepers not to be found."

Although its light has been extinguished and the island it stands on is inundated, this storm-battered tower still stands. Surrounded by water, it can be reached only by boat. Dauphin Island, the closest place to launch a boat, can be reached by driving south from Mobile on State 163.

Abandoned and isolated, Sand Island Light's black tower stands alone in Mobile Bay.

BILOXI LIGHT
Biloxi, Mississippi – 1848

Often located on empty barrier islands or remote spits of sand, lighthouses are frequently isolated and hard to reach. Not so the Biloxi Light. Its white, forty-eight-foot tower sits sandwiched between the eastbound and westbound lanes of U.S. Highway 90.

The brick-and-mortar tower is sheathed in a cast-iron shell. This design has proved a successful one and has enabled the tower to survive countless gulf storms, including the infamous Hurricane Camille in 1968.

In the late 1860s the tower was painted black, and legend has it that this was done as a sign of mourning for President Lincoln. It is an unlikely story, especially when one considers that from the tower you can see Beauvoir, the home of Jefferson Davis who, as president of the Confederacy, was Lincoln's most implacable enemy.

After the Civil War, beach erosion threatened the lighthouse, causing it to lean

a full two feet off the perpendicular. In a desperate attempt to save the structure, workers excavated soil from beneath the tower on the side away from the lean. Almost miraculously, their fight to save the tower succeeded, and it settled back into plumb.

For more than half a century, the Biloxi Lighthouse was kept by a woman. Maria Youghans became keeper in 1867 and only retired in 1920—when her daughter took over the job.

The Biloxi Light stands within sight of Beauvoir, home of Jefferson Davis, president of the Confederacy.

This lighthouse stands in the median strip of US-90 at the foot of Porter Avenue in Biloxi. It is the only lighthouse in the South located on a major highway, and it's right in the middle of it—a marker for motorists as well as seamen.

The tower is now owned and maintained by the city of Biloxi. The lighthouse is open to the public when the weather permits. It is also open at other times by appointment. Weekend tours may be arranged by calling the Biloxi Recreation Department at (601) 435–6293.

NEW CANAL LIGHT
New Orleans, Louisiana – 1838, ca. 1855, and 1892

One of a series of inland lights that mark Louisiana's navigable lakes and bayous, the New Canal Lighthouse stands on the banks of Lake Pontchartrain, several miles north of downtown New Orleans. The lighthouse took its name from an ambitious, though failed, canal-building project begun during the early 1830s. Although the so-called "New Canal" was intended to link Pontchartrain with the New Orleans business district and with the Mississippi River, it was never completed. But while construction continued, a small, bustling harbor developed at the canal's terminus on Lake Pontchartrain.

In 1834 Congress provided $25,000, a considerable sum at that time, for a lighthouse to guide lake traffic in and out of the harbor. The lighthouse was probably made of brick, but despite that and its relatively high cost, it deteriorated rapidly. By 1854 the structure was considered unrepairable and had to be demolished.

It was soon replaced by a cottage-style lighthouse consisting of a lantern on the roof of a keeper's dwelling. Built for only $6,000, this new lighthouse survived the

Civil War and remained in service for more than three decades.

The board discontinued the lighthouse in 1890 and sold the building at public auction. For more than a year the harbor was marked by a lantern hung from a high pole. Meanwhile, workmen erected the two-story, white-frame lighthouse that still stands beside the lake.

Today, only a few traces of the New Canal can be seen, but the lighthouse that bears its name remains active. The building that once doubled as a keeper's dwelling and lighthouse now serves as headquarters for the Coast Guard's Lake Pontchartrain rescue service. Answering more than 300 search-and-rescue calls per year, it is the busiest Coast Guard Station in the world.

Take I–10 and I–610 to the West End Boulevard North exit. Then take West End Boulevard to Lake Shore Boulevard and Lake Pontchar-train. The lighthouse is visible from Lake Shore Boulevard. Tours can be arranged with the Coast Guard by calling (504) 589–2331. Advanced notice is recommended.

The New Canal Light on Lake Pontchartrain has been active since 1838.

BOLIVAR POINT LIGHT
Near Galveston, Texas – 1852 and 1872

Built in 1852, the original Bolivar Point Light was constructed of cast-iron sections that raised the lantern more than 100 feet above sea level. When the Civil War broke out, the Confederates pulled down the tower and reforged the iron, apparently using it to make weapons. Reconstruction of the lighthouse following the war was cut short by a yellow-fever epidemic that caused the government to place several hundred miles of the Texas coast under quarantine.

The new lighthouse, erected at a cost of more than $50,000 by work crews brought in from New Orleans, was not completed until late 1872. Like its predecessor and the lighthouse at Biloxi, the tower had an iron shell. This greatly increased the strength of the tower, enabling it to survive numerous gales, such as the disastrous hurricane in 1900 (described in the introduction to this chapter).

In 1915 another hurricane bore down on Galveston, and once more, the Bolivar Point Lighthouse became a refuge. This time about sixty people climbed onto the tower steps to escape the wind and the flood tide accompanying the storm. The flood carried away the tank containing the oil supply for the lamps so that the light was extinguished for two critical days following the storm.

Discontinued by the Coast Guard in 1933, the Bolivar Point Light has been dark now for more than half a century.

Now privately owned and closed to the public, the tower can be seen from State 87 on the Bolivar Peninsula. To reach the peninsula, take the free ferry from the north end of Galveston Island. The ferry provides an excellent view of the lighthouse.

The Bolivar Point Light survived a severe hurricane on the Gulf of Mexico in 1900.

POINT ISABEL LIGHT
Point Isabel, Texas – 1852

Also constructed in 1852, a good year for lighthouses in Texas, the Point Isabel Light was erected on an old army camp used by the forces of General Zachary Taylor during the Mexican War. The site also attracted considerable military interest during the Civil War. Both the Confederate and Northern forces used the tower as an observation post, and on May 13, 1865, the two sides fought each other at Palmito Ranch, almost within a rifle shot of the lighthouse. The Southerners won the battle but discovered, to their dismay, that they had already lost the war. Robert E. Lee had surrendered at Appomattox Courthouse in Virginia more than a month earlier.

Sea traffic in the vicinity of Port Isabel began to decline after the war, and in 1888 the Lighthouse Board discontinued the light. A few years later, when board members voted to re-exhibit the light, they were very surprised to learn that the government no longer owned the lighthouse. Technically speaking, the government had never owned Point Isabel itself. It seems that General Taylor had not

purchased the land but had illegally expropriated it for the use of his army. After years of litigation and negotiation, the board ended up having to buy back its own lighthouse from a Texas rancher for $6,000.

Shortly after the turn of the century, the Point Isabel Light fell permanently dark. Although not used for more than eighty years, it remains in excellent condition, the centerpiece, in fact, of Texas's smallest state park.

The lighthouse stands on a hill beside State 100 just east of the junction with State 48 in the center of Port Isabel. The state of Texas maintains the lighthouse. There are self-guided tours daily.

For more information, contact the Texas Parks and Wildlife Department, 4200 Smith School Road, Austin, Texas 78744; (210) 943–1172.

Point Isabel Light has stood for nearly 140 years.

BIBLIOGRAPHY

Adams, William Henry Davenport. *Lighthouses and Lightships: A Descriptive and Historical Account of Their Mode of Construction and Organization.* New York: Scribner's, 1870.

Adamson, Hans Christian. *Keepers of the Light.* New York: Greenberg, 1955.

Beaver, Patrick. *A History of Lighthouses.* Secaucus, N.J.: Citadel, 1972.

Buehr, Walter. *Storm Warning: The Story of Hurricanes and Tornadoes.* New York: Morrow, 1972.

Chase, Mary Ellen. *The Story of Lighthouses.* New York: Norton, 1965.

Cipra, David L. *Lighthouses and Lightships of the Gulf of Mexico.* U.S. Coast Guard, 1978.

Conway, Martin. *The Outer Banks: An Historical Adventure from Kitty Hawk to Ocracoke.* Shepherdstown, W.V.: Carabelle Books, 1985.

Dean, Love. *Reef Lights: Seaswept Lighthouses of the Florida Keys.* Key West: The Historic Key West Preservation Board, 1982.

De Wire, Elinore. *Florida Lighthouses.*

DuBois, Bessie Wilson. "Jupiter Lighthouse." *The Journal of the Historical Association of Southern Florida* 20 (1960).

de Gast, Robert. *The Lighthouses of the Chesapeake.* Baltimore: Johns Hopkins University, 1973.

Holland, Francis Ross, Jr. *America's Lighthouses: Their Illustrated History Since 1716.* Brattleboro, Vt.: Stephen Greene Press, 1972.

Kagerer, Rudy. *A Guidebook to Lighthouses: In South Carolina, Georgia, and Florida's East Coast.* Athens, Ga.: Lighthouse Enterprises, 1985.

Marx, Robert. *Shipwrecks of the Western Hemisphere.* New York: David McKay Company, 1971.

Mason, Herbert Mollow. *Death from the Seas: The Galveston Hurricane of 1900.* New York: Dial, 1972.

McCormick, William Henry. *The Modern Book of Lighthouses, Lifeboats, and Lightships.* London: W. Heinemann, 1913.

Moe, Christine. *Lighthouses and Lightships.* Monticello, Ill.: 1979.

Naush, John M. *Seamarks: Their History and Development.* London: Stanford Maritime, 1985.

Parker, Tony. *Lighthouse.* New York: Taplinger, 1976.

Pouliot, Richard, and Julie Pouliot. *Shipwrecks on the Virginia Coast.* Centreville, Md.: Tidewater, 1986.

Scheina, Robert L. "The Evolution of the Lighthouse Tower," *Lighthouses: Then and Now* (supplement to the U.S. Coast Guard Commandant's Bulletin).

Shomette, Donald. *Shipwrecks on the Chesapeake.* Centreville, Md.: Tidewater, 1982.

Simpson, Robert. *The Hurricane and Its Impact.* Baton Rouge: Louisiana State University, 1980.

Snowe, Edward Rowe, *Famous Lighthouses of America.* New York: Dodd, Mead, 1955.

———— *Great Gales and Dire Disasters.* New York: Dodd, Mead, 1952.

Stick, David. *North Carolina Lighthouses.* Raleigh, N.C.: North Carolina Department of Cultural Resources, 1980.

Talbot, Frederick Arthur Ambrose. *Lightships and Lighthouses.* London: W. Heinemann, 1913.

Tate, Suzanne. *Whalehead: Tales of Corolla, N.C.* Nags Head, N.C.: Nags Head Art, 1987.

United States Coast Guard. *Historically Famous Lighthouses.* CG-232, 1986.

———— *Chronology of Aids to Navigation and the Old Lighthouse Service.* CG 458, 1974.

Weiss, George. *The Lighthouse Service: Its History, Activities and Organization.* Baltimore: Johns Hopkins University, 1926.

Witney, Dudley. *The Lighthouse.* Boston: New York Graphic Society, 1975.

INDEX

PHOTO INFORMATION

The photographs in this book were taken on Fuji chrome color film and T-MAX black-and-white film. Other films, I'm sure, would have worked just as well; but being a travel photographer who takes trips constantly, I've learned to simplify what I take in my camera bag. The typical contents include two Nikon 8008 camera bodies with a small assortment of lenses: a 24-mm wide angle, a 35-135-mm zoom, a short telephoto lens such as an f2 85 mm, and a longer 70-300-mm zoom. Then there's my tripod; yes, *tripod*. When I was a young newspaper photographer, I thought tripods were for novice photographers who were afraid to blur images. Now I think only the overconfident do *not* use them. And for lighthouses, a tripod is a necessity unless you want only full-daylight pictures. In addition, there are in my camera case two little pieces of glass that I'm always looking for, and one or the other will be on my camera lens most of the time when I am shooting. One is a polarizing filter that enhances the color in bright, sunlit shots; the other is a warming filter that prevents the bluish cast that occurs on cloudy days and in deep shade on sunny days.

The photograph of Cape St. George Light on page 95 exemplifies the effect of a polarizing filter. The deep blue sky and rich color in the sea oats have been enhanced by the filter. It is easy to use; place it on the lens and rotate it until the color looks best. The camera meter automatically adjusts the exposure.

The picture of Hatteras at night on the cover was a four-second time exposure with the camera on a tripod with the legs stuck in the wet sand. Right after a wave recedes, the sand is wet and acts like a mirror, and with some luck you can make this fleeting mirror reflect the beacon's light.

There are two light shows, sunrise and dusk, at every lighthouse each day; these are the coveted times I like to be shooting. At most working lighthouses the light comes on half an hour before sunset and stays on for half an hour after sunrise, giving photographs an opportunity to work with the beacon's light shining. See the Hilton Head Light photo on page 47 for an example. Also look at the Currituck Beach Light on page 31. This is the effect of late-evening photography.

When photographing lighthouses, look for details such as the stairways on page 65. Doorways, cornerstone dates, and windows all make good detail shots. At lighthouses where you can tour inside, objects and artifacts such as a coffeepot and cup add interest, as exemplified in the photo on page 13.

A lighthouse's beam of light will look brighter if you can get a high elevation with your camera. Remember, the Fresnel lens is concentrating the light into a narrow beam; if you are standing at the base of the light, that beam is far above your head. Back off several hundred feet; the light will look a great deal more intense.

Try walking around the lighthouse, if possible, and viewing it from *all* the compass points. You may like one of the less-photographed points of view better than the usual angle. Remember, there is no "right" and "wrong" way to photograph a lighthouse. It's your film and imagination. Do it any way you like.

—BRUCE ROBERTS

ABOUT THE AUTHORS

BRUCE ROBERTS and his wife, Cheryl, who helped with the research for this book, live on North Carolina's Outer Banks, not far from the Bodie Island Lighthouse. For many years Bruce was Senior Travel Photographer for *Southern Living* magazine. He started his career working as a photographer for newspapers in Tampa, Florida, and Charlotte, North Carolina. He is the recipient of many photography awards, and some of his photos are in the permanent collection of the Smithsonian Institution. Recently Bruce and Cheryl opened the Lighthouse Gallery & Gifts, a store devoted to lighthouse books, artifacts, and collectibles, in Nags Head.

RAY JONES is a freelance writer living in Washington, D.C.. He has been a text editor for Time-Life Books, an editor at *Albuquerque Living,* and a writing coach and senior editor at *Southern Living Magazine.* Mr. Jones grew up in Macon, Georgia, was inspired by the writing of Faulkner and Hemingway, and worked his way through college as a disc jockey. He holds a B.A. in history and political science and has completed postgraduate work in literature, nonfiction writing, and philosophy.